Freedom Movement In India 1857-1947

Suresh Chandra Ghosh

Originals
Delhi-110052

First Published 1991
Second Edition 2011

ISBN 13: 978-81-8454-107-6
ISBN 10: 81-8454-107-4

Published by
Originals
A-6, Nimri Commercial Centre,
Ashok Vihar Phase-IV, Delhi-110052
Phones: 27302453
e-mail: info@Lppindia.com
url: www.Lppindia.com

Printed at
D K Fine Art Press P Ltd.
Delhi-110052

PRINTED IN INDIA

Contents

Section III

The Climactic Years, 1918-47

Preface to the Second Edition

The book was first published in 1991 by Arnold India. Immediately after its publication, I began to receive letters from its readers via my publisher from places as far as Chennai, Mumbai, Kolkata and Bangalore appreciating the work. This is possibly because of the treatment of the subject which I have analysed chronologically, episode by episode, briefly but substantially, in terms of cause and effect relationship, for a clear understanding of the progress in the movement for our freedom.

The book was sold out within two years after its publication. A second reprint could not be brought out as the publisher, for reasons not known to me, closed its business in India. And as I was too busy first with my research on history of education and then with my visit to Friedrich Schiller Univesitat, Jena, Germany, where I lectured on the emergence of our education system from our religious scriptures in ancient India, followed by its publication by Peter Lang at Frankfurt in 2002, the idea of bringing out a second edition did not occur to me. It is only after my retirement in August 2002 that I began to think of it. However, a request for a contribution to NCERT's Encyclopedia of Indian Education followed by another from Routledge to its International Encyclopedia of Education as well as my preoccupation with bringing out the third edition of my book on history of education in modern India by Orient Black Swan, delayed it further. I am now grateful to Mr. Pradeep Mittal of Originals,New Delhi, for his offer to bring out its second edition just at a time when the Indian National Congress is celebrating the 125 years of its existence.

The book was originally written for a non-specialist audience keeping in mind the interests of the Senior Secondary and Undergraduate students in history but I was pleasantly surprised to find while obtaining a xerox copy of the book from the Text Book Section of the JNU Library that it has also been extensively used by our history students at the Master's degree level. An Introduction highlighting the genesis of our Freedom Movement in the mounting unemployment among the Western educated youth since 1857 and a Post script illuminating the psychological factor which contributes to the inevitability of the partition of our country have been added to the second edition. It is hoped the second edition of the book will receive the same appreciation from its readers as it has been bestowed on it earlier.

Suresh Chandra Ghosh

Introduction

We have started our account of the Freedom Movement with the year 1857, when groups of people consisting of princes and feudal lords whose interests were affected badly by the rule of the East Company joined the Sepoys who had risen against it. The young and the Western educated Indians of the metropolitan cities who had benefited from the rule of the Company, had now opportunities for employment in the lower levels of the Company's administration as well as in other European establishments that were then coming into existence to meet the increasing needs and requirements of a growing European communities, kept themselves aloof from the nightmarish incident. Paradoxically enough, it is these young Western educated Indians who later provided the leadership of the movement and carried it to its fulfillment after years of toils and turmoils, sorrows and sufferings in 1947.

These young men were the products of the Western education, ideas and values which accompanied the introduction of English education in the country by Bentinck in March 1835 and true to the observation of Macaulay who counselled Bentinck on the subject in February 1835, became "a class of persons Indian in blood and colour, but English in taste, in opinions, in morals and intellect" and served as the interpreters between the rulers and the ruled. However, Bentinck who was imbued with the utilitarian philosophy of Bentham and Mill and was driven by an urge to strip the Indian society of its evils and vices such as sati, infanticide and child-marriage as well as to modernise it, was also conscious same time, as revealed in one of his letters written to Mancy on 1 June 1834,of the subtle danger and risk inherent in the spread of Western education and ideas among a community of people long used to live as "Zimmis" or as protected subjects on payment of a poll tax called Jizya, for centuries under the rule of Islam which began in 1206. He wrote: "I cannot regard the advantage of ignorance to the governors or the governed. If our rule is bad, as I believe it to be, let the natives have the means through knowledge, to represent their grievances and to obtain redress." These means, Bentinck thought, could only be acquired by a spread of Western education and ideas, knowledge and science and to that end, he began working immediately after coming to India as Governor-General in 1828. His first step was to gradually introduce the use of the English language replacing Persian in all governmental works.

However as far as the "natives" were concerned, they could have the means to dispel their "ignorance" and to obtain "redress" for their grievances only when they were able to educate themselves in institutions offering English education. By 1834 the missionaries had opened schools in the metropolitan cities of the country and among them Alexander Duff's General Assembly Institution at Calcutta, now known as the Scottish Church College, was remarkable in offering a course on English education to the higher classes of the contemporary society. The Indians in collaboration with the benevolent watch-maker David Hare had earlier set up the Hindu School in 1817, which had by now become the Hindu College. By the time Bentinck wrote this letter to Mancy, English classes were already attached to the government supported Calcutta Madrasah, Delhi College, Agra College under pressure from Home and now they were attached to the Benares Sanskrit College as a mark of respect for Bentinck's wishes.

The number of such institutions offering English classes considerably increased after Bentinck passed the official order on English education in March 1835 and soon after the universities at Calcutta, Bombay and Madras came into existence in 1857, their number rose from 27 to 72 in 1880-1881 by leaps and bounds particularly in the metropolitan cities of the country. And also there was now a gradual increase annually in the number of educated Indians at the matriculation and the graduate levels who could not be absorbed in the administration of the country. The higher positions both in the civil and the military administration were reserved for the British recruits at London and though the Civil Service was thrown open to the Indians in 1853, few could afford to go to London to take the examination for it.

There was a growing discontent and disillusionment among the increasing number of the unemployed educated Indians "who once appeared to receive their honours in the university convocation now applying for some lowly-paid appointment, almost begging from office to office, from department to department, or struggling for the practice of a petty practitioner, and after all this returning baffled and disheartened to a poverty-stricken home." And soon imbued with Western education, ideas and values, the educated unemployed began to resort to "the use of the Western method of agitation and organization acquired through the universities and the colleges" and their first landmark opportunity came when Surendra Nath Banerjea organised a protest through the Indian Association he had set up in 1876, against the reduction of the upper age-limit from 21 to 19, at which the Indian Civil Service Examination could be taken at London, which received the warmest support from the educated Indians throughout the country. Such an agitation organised on a Western model posed "a real danger" to the British rule in India and the British officials were quick to realise that it was rooted in the spread of the Western education in the country.

With this realisation the British Government in India tried to put the clock back and arrest the progress of the higher education in the country and their first step was to appoint the Hunter Commission on education in 1882 under Sir William Hunter. Hunter who was advised to recommend the withdrawal of the who was advised to recommend the withdrawal of the governmental support from the field of secondary and collegiate education, felt that the government supported education was producing among the educated Indians, a sense of revolt against the three principles which represented "the deepest wants of human nature–the principle of discipline, the principle of religion, the principle of contentment." Ripon who appointed the Hunter Commission observed rather sympathetically for the educated Indians in his Convocation Address at the University of Bombay in 1884: "It is little short of folly that we should throw open to increasing numbers the rich stores of Western learning: that we should inspire them with European ideas, and bring them into the closest contact with English thought, and that then we should as it were, pay no heed to the growth of those aspirations which we have ourselves created and the pride of those ambitions we have ourselves called forth."

An outlet for discharging the steam of discontent which had been gathering in the minds of the unemployed educated Indians for some time past against the British administration was needed and this was found in the formation of the Indian National Congress as "a safety valve" by a former civilian, Allan Octavian Hume, now living in Simla, with an active support from Dufferin in 1885. The Indian National Congress adopted "wider employment of our people in the public service" as one of "the three important questions" constituting "the chief planks in the Congress platform" and hardly any annual session of the Indian National Congress took place without discussing the subject of employment and passing resolutions on it.

The year of the formation of the Indian National Congress is the real starting point of our struggle for freedom though freedom was not then very much in the mind of the organizers and members of the Congress. What the members of the Indian National Congress wanted at the moment was a constitutional reform to let them have a share in the administration of the country. They met annually every year in the month of December and prayed and

The net result of the Congress Sessions held till the early 1890s was the passing of the Act of 1892 which did not satisfy its members. Obviously a section of the Indian National Congress lost its patience and resorted to active hostility against the British administration. When, within ten days of Tilak's Shivaji festival on 12 June 1897, two British plague officers of Poona, Rand and his associate, Lt.Ayerst were murdered for their atrocities committed on the people, by the two educated but unemployed former students of the Ferguson College, Damodar and Balkrishna Chapekar, the British Government confirmed its earlier diagnosis that the root of the problem lay at the spread of Western education and ideas and that the decision to promote English education since the days of Macaulay "was a story of grave political miscalculation." However it was not too late to rectify this error and could possibly be done by tightening the grip of the government on higher education in the country. With that end in view, Curzon summoned a Conference at Simla in 1901, where he thus commented on the spread of the English education in the country: "When Erasmus was reproached with having laid the egg from which came forth the Reformation, 'Yes', he replied: 'but I laid a hen's egg, and Luther has hatched a fighting cock.'" Curzon passed in 1902 the Indian Universities Act on the pretext of reforming the five existing universities including the three set up at Calcutta, Bombay and Madras in the year of the Rising of the Sepoys, to bring them under the full control of the government.

However, the members of the Indian National Congress were quick to realize that the real motif was to control the spread of higher education in the country and led by Surendra Nath Banerjea of Bengal unleashed an agitation against it in almost all the metropolitan cities of the country. This alarmed the government and since Bengal was the scene of most of the anti-British activities, the former quickly chalked out a plan to circumcise it by partitioning it in such a way as to have the Muslim dominated areas in one major part in Eastern Bengal to create a separate entity for use as a bulwark against the anti-partition agitators of the Western and major part in Eastern Bengal to create a separate entity for use as a bulwark against the anti-partition agitators of the Western and other parts. The Bengal was partitioned in 1905 and the act represented the climax of the British policy of divide and rule which began in the early nineteenth century when on the eve of the passing of the Charter Act of 1813 the senior officials of the East India Company argued against the dispatch of the Christian missionaries to India for proselytisation fearing an united resistance by the Hindus and the Muslims to the Company's administration in India. The move to partition Bengal in 1905 was indeed successful for it gave birth to the Muslim League next year, which not only supported the partition of Bengal at the moment but in future it became a tool in the hands of the British to thwart the Congress interests and ideas and some four decades later it became a monster to grab a portion of the sub-continent as Pakistan.

This is the crystallized view of the freedom movement in our country and since each episode of the movement has been delineated very briefly but substantially, discussed and analysed chronologically in terms of cause and effect relationship which subtly flows underneath each development, in the pages of the book, it is not necessary here to enter into details of the movement.

Yet on the basis of what little has been said above, it is clear that the freedom movement stewarded by the Indian National Congress has absolutely little or no relevance to the year 1857 except the fact that it saw the establishment of three universities on the London model in the three metropolitan cities—Calcutta, Bombay and Madras and these three universities provided the continuous feed back to the movement in respect of its educated personnel and ideas. The vision and goals of the participants in the Rising of the Sepoys were absolutely different from those of the educated professional classes who formed the backbone of the Indian National Congress. The affected groups who revolted against the British administration in 1857 wanted to restore their old medieval feudal glory and order, power and privileges and had no idea of a larger vision of a progressive and modernized, united and independent country of the educated members of the Indian National Congress and its supporters.

Still there are people and scholars in the country who describe the Rising of the Sepoys in 1857 as the First War of Independence. The basis for such a description is very unclear. The Rising of the Sepoys was no doubt a war against the British but if it is the First War of Independence, should we then call the freedom movement which was , except for a brief interlude under the extremist leaders like Lajpat Rai, Bal Gangadhar Tilak and Bipin Chandra Pal, mostly non-violent and passive as guided by Surendra Nath Banerjea, Pherozeshah Mehta, G.K.Gokhale, M.K.Gandhi, Nehru and Patel as the Second War of Independence? If there had been at all a War of Independence against the British, it happened towards the withering stage of Gandhi's Quit India Movement. And the credit for organizing this war should go to Gandhi's rebel in the Congress, Netaji Subhas Chandra Bose and his Azad Hind Fauz which backed by the Japanese army advanced through Burma as far as Imphal in June 1944. It eventually surrendered to the British forces and because of its failure to achieve its goal nobody among us perhaps gives it the adequate importance it deserves.

Secondly, there has been no continuity between the Rising of the Sepoys in 1857 and the emergence of the Indian National Congress in 1885 either in the form of persons or in the form of events and ideas. The events preceding the formation of the Indian National Congress had nothing to do with the event of 1857 and the persons involved in them were the Western educated Indians who had earlier kept themselves aloof from the Rising of the Sepoys as they saw the British connexion as the gateway to the modernisation of their country.

For example, the educated Indians as well as some enlightened Englishmen supported the agitation of the peasants against the exploitation by the indigo planters, which took place immediately after 1857 but none of the living participants in the Rising of the

Sepoys could be seen among the former. The political associations by Dadabhai Naoroji in 1866,by Ranade, Gokhale, Joshi, Chiplunkar and Deshpande in 1867,by Surendranath Banerjea in 1876 had nothing to with the kind of interests and goals which guided the Rising of the Sepoys in 1857.These associations were initially formed with the idea of persuading the British Government to honour the successive pledges of justice and fair play made in the Charter Acts of 1833, 1853 and the Queen's Proclamation of 1858, which were never implemented much to the disappointment and despair of the educated Indians who had earlier supported the British administration against the revolt of the Sepoys and the allied groups.

As a matter of fact, Banerjea's Indian Association came very near to the Indian National Congress which later put Swaraj as a goal. In its inaugural address at the Albert Hall in Calcutta on 26 July 1876, Banerjea declared his Indian Association was to be "the centre of an all-India movement" based on "the conception of a united India, derived from the inspiration of Mazzini," who was the architect of the recent unification of Italy. It was Banerjea's Indian Association which provided a successful leadership in the agitation against the Civil Service and the Vernacular Press Act in 1876-1879 and organized a National Conference which held its first and second meetings at Calcutta in December 1883 and 1885 respectively and after one year in 1886 it merged with the Indian National Congress at its Calcutta session under the presidentship of Dadabhai Naoroji.

Clearly none of these organizations and the associations mentioned above reflected the motives and interests of the participants in the Rising of the Sepoys in 1857. For those who led and gave up their lives in the course of the freedom movement, it remained an isolated event and very rarely found any mention in any of the proceedings of the sessions of the Indian National Congress since 1885. The significance of the Rising of the Sepoys in 1857 lies not so much in inspiring a freedom movement to the educated Indians but in ushering a change in the policy and the

We have achieved our freedom in 1947. However, it is not the kind of freedom as had been originally visualized by our national leaders beginning with Surendra Nath Banerjea and the debate is still going on the extent of the responsibility of our national leaders vis-a-vis the British Government for the partition of our country. Debate is also going on whether the bifurcation of India has been a curse or a blessing. We propose to attend to this debate very briefly at the end of our account of the movement in the form of a Postscript.

Finally, the work as stated in the Preface was first published in 1991 and though primarily meant for a non-specialist audience and the students of history at the Senior Secondary and the Undergraduate levels is based on an extensive use of the Proceedings of the Indian National Congress as available at the Nehru Memorial Museum and Library, Teen Murti House, New Delhi and the contemporary newspapers as available at the News papers Section of the National Library, Esplanade, Calcutta, as well as the contemporary memoirs, diaries and other printed works available on the subject during our period. The Private Papers of those Viceroys and Governor-Generals which are available on microfilm at the Nehru Memorial Museum and Library as well as at the National Archives, New Delhi were also consulted. A Select Bibliography including the pre- and post-1947 publications of some authentic works on the subject has been added at the end for those who may be further interested in it.

Section I
The Pre-Congress Years, 1857-1885

Chapter 1

Eighteen Fifty-Seven

On a hot summer day of 10 May 1857, a group of sepoys were galloping towards Delhi. They were the sepoys from Meerut who had murdered their European officers, burnt their houses and released their imprisoned colleagues just a few hours ago. On reaching Delhi they were joined by the sepoys stationed there, seized the city and by nightfall declared the aged Bahadur Shah II, the titular Mughal Emperor, as the Emperor of Hindustan. On 11 May as the British Commander-in-Chief, General Anson, was collecting troops and transport at Ambala to reach Delhi, the sepoys at Nasirabad in Rajputana, Nimach in Gwalior, at Lucknow, Cawnpore, and Benares in the United Provinces, rose together with the Rani of Jhansi in Bundelkhand. And by mid-June the British authority from the borders of Rajputana to the neighbourhood of Patna in Bihar had practically ceased to exist.

The sepoys belonged to the Bengal Army which consisted of recruits from highcaste men in Oudh and the North-Western Provinces. They revolted because they were asked to use the cartridges for the newly introduced Enfield rifle which were said to be smeared with the fat of cows and pigs. This outraged the feelings of both Hindu sepoys to whom the cow was sacred and Muslim sepoys to whom the pig was unclean. They now shared the general suspicion of the Indian people as to the Westernising and Christianising policy of the British Raj. This suspicion was more than confirmed when Canning passed the General Service Enlistment Act under which all recruits to the Bengal Army were ordered to be ready for service both within and outside India. An engagement outside India after crossing the Black Water would make them outcastes in the eyes of the Indian society and would not the missionaries then step in to convert them into Christianity? They had already mutineed on four occasions before May 1857 as their demand for extra allowances for fighting in remote regions in India had not been met and now that a large proportion of British troops had been withdrawn for service, in several extra-Indian wars like the Crimean War, the Persian War and the Chinese War, was not the moment opportune for a war against the *Mlechhas ?*

Yet what looked like a revolt of the sepoys at the start, soon became a revolt of the large section of the Indian people adversely affected by a past century of British administration in India. Dalhousie's policy of annexation had alarmed the whole princely order and their dependants. Each state annexed and each court extinguished for misgovernment or lack of a natural successor meant, perhaps, the removal of a centre of oppression and corruption. But it meant also further contraction of the area where Indians could hold high office, where men of good family could look forward to a career of honour in the public service. It meant also the creation of another group of resentful and perhaps desperate people who would seize any opportunity of expressing their feelings which might come their way. The Rani of Jhansi and her followers were one of these because she believed that she had been robbed of her ruling rights in defiance of recognized Hindu law. So also was the Nana Sahib at Bithur because he thought that he had a claim to the title of Peshwa and the pension of Baji Rao. The princely circle of Delhi caught the fever of unrest from events around them in anticipation of the lapse of the imperial title and the removal of the Mughal family to Mehrauli. The Oudh *Taluqdars* saw danger to their estates as well as to their political position when Coverley Jackson who succeeded James Outram fanned their fears by disbanding the royal army and starting inquiries into *Taluqdari* titles.

These political fears were supplemented by the alarm felt by the whole order of large landholders. The Permanent Settlement in Bengal had displaced many old established *Zamindari* families since 1793 but created in its place new families who became after two generations well-established and firm supporters of the British Raj. However, Bentinck's resumption of rent free tenures dispossessed many among them for no other reason than loss of title deeds and left them with a sense of grievance. During the five years before the outbreak in 1857, the Inam Commission at Bombay, appointed by Dalhousie to investigate the titles of landowners confiscated some 20,000 estates in the Deccan, without considering for a moment that such a drastic measure was sure to create complications in the economic condition of the country.

A large section of the people were really alarmed at the rapid spread of Western civilisation in India in the first half of the nineteenth century. Since 1813 the missionaries had been allowed to come and preach Christianity. *Sati* had been legally banned in 1829 and infanticide abolished and in 1835 English had replaced Persian as the official language. With the coming of Dalhousie as the Governor-General in 1848 came the railways and the electric telegraph and the former innovation delivered cruel blows to the caste system in India by compelling an upper caste, say, a sacred Brahmin, to travel in the same compartment with a fellow traveller who was possibly a *Dome* or a *Sudra*, the mere sight or contact of one was sufficient to entail a loss of caste. Dalhousie's successor, Canning in 1856 legally permitted the widows to remarry and the converts from Hinduism to inherit property. Was not this evidence of a design to subvert the ancient religion? Already the emergence of a group of Westernised young men in the chief metropolitan cities of British India had created enough consternation among the conservative Indians and now they wondered with great alarm at the real intention of the British Raj—was it to Westernise their land at the cost of their time-honoured customs and practices and to convert India to Christianity? As we have already said the sepoys whose discontent was regularly fanned by the disgruntled princes and landholders and all those affected by the British land revenue system shared this suspicion. On this inflammable material the true story of the greased cartridges fell as a spark and the whole country from the Sutlej to the Narmada was ablaze.

It is not necessary to enter here into a detailed description of the course of the revolt. It may be briefly mentioned here that Delhi, the loss of which was a blow to the prestige of the British Raj in India was recovered on 20 September 1857 and on 1 March 1858, Colin Campbell, joining forcess with Outram, recovered Lucknow and pressed the remnants of the rebel forces back into the Terai bordering Nepal. Nana Sahib went with them and disappeared in the border jungles. It was in Central India that the reckless courage of Lakshmi Bai, the Rani of Jhansi and the skill of Tantia Topi relieved the gloom of a hopeless struggle. On 17 June 1858, the Rani of Jhansi attired in a soldier's dress met a soldier's end and Tantia Topi was chased from place to place till early next year when he was captured and hanged. Canning proclaimed peace on 8 July 1858 throughout India and despite the clamour for vengeance, arranged for the proper trial and punishment of those only who were really guilty. Bahadur Shah who was taken prisoner after the recapture of Delhi was deported to Rangoon, where he spent his last days in exile, till he died in 1862, at the age of eighty-seven.

For the sepoys of Meerut who marched to Delhi and proclaimed Bahadur Shah II as the Emperor of Hindustan, for the sepoys of other places who rose against their European masters and finally for the Oudh *Talukdars,* the Jhansi *Sardars,* the Nana's circle, the Mughal princes, the Maulvi of Fyzebad and Kunwar Singh of Bihar, the outbreak of 1857 was certainly a war of independence. It was an occasion when Hindus and Muslims, despite their religions, had united to fight a common enemy with a common object. The common enemy was the British Raj and the common object was a return to the pre-British days. However, the rebels were so steeped in the medieval ways of thinking that the whole affair assumed in their minds a purely personal aspect. Elimination of foreign rule was equated with the physical destruction of the foreign personnel and independence identified with the restoration of the personal rule of those deprived of their rights and privileges by the British Raj. There was no doubt that the revolt, if successful, would have restored the old days of the Mughal rule and brought to an abrupt halt the process of modernization started by the British Raj. This was one thing which the Westernised Indians of the metropolitan cities of British India and many among the Indian rulers and statesmen like Sindhia and his minister, Dinkar Rao, Salar Jang, the minister of Hyderabad, the Begam of Bhopal, Jang Bahadur, the able minister of Napal, the Sikh Sardars, Gulab Singh of Kashmir and Dost Muhammad of Afghanistan did not like. They not only remained loyal to the British Raj but helped the administration to arrest the spread of the outbreak.

The rebels were thus mostly inspired by passions which centred in their grievances, and not on any larger ideals. So they gained little advantage from initial successes and nothing but despair from their defeats. Where the populace joined in, as round Saharanpur and Bareilly, it was on account of particular grievances rather than from any larger vision of a new India. Those who had any such vision, as had some muslims and the Nana Sahib's circle, looked backwards rather than forward with the result that their programmes clashed. Except the Rani of Jhansi, Tantia Topi and Kunwar Singh, the rebels could not boast of any other leader to direct them to glory. The British, on the other hand, enjoyed gifted and determined leadership, and possessed a compact discipline based upon a robust national pride. They had a long record of success and the hope of reinforcements to sustain them against heavy odds. And finally they had abounding self confidence springing from the belief that they represented the irrestible forces of progress in the modern world.

So the failute of the outbreak of 1857 was almost a foregone conclusion. Yet it must be admitted that the outbreak posed a major challenge to the British rule in India and the cause for which the rebels, Hindus and Muslims, fought and gave up their lives was not unjust though its ethos was inadequate. They wanted to free their territories from an alien rule but failed to achieve the object. In the ultimate analysis, the outbreak of 1857 was the last attempt of an effete order to recover its lost glory. With its defeat at the hands of the British, the ground was cleared for the emergence of the new forces which dominated the history of India for the next ninety years.

Chapter 2

Blue Mutiny

The outbreak of 1857 was followed by the transfer of power from the Company to the Crown when on 2 August 1858 an "Act for the Better Government of India" was passed by the British Parliament. The Act provided that "India shall be governed by, and in the name of the Sovereign through one of the principal Secretaries of State, assisted by a council of fifteen members". The assumption of the Government of India by the Sovereign of Great Britain was announced by Canning on 1 November 1858 at a darbar at Allahabad in a proclamation issued in the name of the Queen. The Queen's Proclamation while confirming the treaties of the East India Company with the Indian princes promised to respect their rights and privileges, disclaimed all desire for British territorial expansion in India at their cost and pardoned all offenders except those really found guilty of murdering the British subjects in 1857. It promised to respect the ancient rights, usages and customs of India and to abstain from any interference with Indian religion and proclaimed that all those found eligible by education, ability and integrity would be freely admitted to offices in the service of the British Raj, irrespective of race or creed.

It is clear the Queen's Proclamation wanted to avoid a repetition of 1857 by removing the grievances of the princes and the orthodox Indians that led to the outbreak. This was further confirmed by an immediate reorganisation of the army strengthening the European element both at the officer's and soldier's level. However, the Queen's Proclamation did not indicate any change in the policy of the East India Company towards the peasantry who participated in large numbers in the outbreak particularly in Bihar and the United Provinces. The peasantry in India bore the main brunt of colonial exploitation. They suffered under the land revenue systems—*Zamindari and Ryotwari*—introduced by the British Raj. Because of the high revenue rates and the rigid manner of collection, the peasant had often to borrow money with exorbitant interest from the money lender to pay taxes. Besides paying taxes, the peasant had to borrow when crops failed in times of droughts, floods and famines from the money lender who could manipulate the judicial and administrative system introduced by the British to his advantage. The vicious system of exploitation of the peasantry was vividly revealed when the humble Bengali cultivators rose against the European indigo planters in the autumn of 1859.

The European indigo planters used to keep the cultivators in a state of complete dependence and forced them to cultivate the crop against their will as its cultivation had become increasingly unprofitable to them. The misdeeds of the planters and the suffering of the cultivators had become well-known in the villages and towns of Bengal. Backed by the more influential sections of the rural Bengali society, the cultivators in the district of Murshidabad formed "a regular league" against indigo cultivation. While travelling by steamer in the Pabna district in September 1860, J.P. Grant, the Lt. Governor of Bengal, was surprised by the orderly demonstration made by the cultivators including their wives and children against indigo cultivation and was much impressed by their organization and capacity for combined and simultaneous action. Canning was afraid that "a shot fired in anger or fear by a foolish planter might put every factory in Lower Bengal in flames".

The Blue Mutiny, as it was called, spread from one indigo district to another and involved thousands of cultivators, Hindus and Muslims. It remained largely non-violent, though marked by a few occasional armed clashes. Threatened with financial ruin, the indigo planters approached the mercantile community of Calcutta for help. And the British Raj, torn between its sympathy for the European planters and its obligation towards the oppressed cultivators, issued a notification telling the cultivators that they were not obliged to enter into contracts for the cultivation of indigo though the existing contracts for the purpose must be fulfilled. The Raj set up a special commission of inquiry which reinforced the case of the cultivators and their friends against the planters.

It is interesting to note that the case of the indigo cultivators were supported not only by the educated Indians including certain progressive zamindars but also by some Christian missionaries and British officials despite the ill-feelings and hatred between the two races aggravated by the excesses of the outbreak in 1857. When the Rev. James Long was tried and convicted for his part in the English translation of *Nil Darpan,* a satirical Bengali play by Dinabandhu Mitra directed against the indigo planters, he became a sort of martyr in the eyes of the Indians. An Indian paid his fine and when in 1861 Long left for England, a deputation of Indians under Raja Radhakanta Deb waited on him and expressed gratitude for his conduct.

The significance of the Blue Mutiny which struck a hard blow at the tyranny and exploitation practised by the indigo planters was never lost on the educated Indians. It taught them the value of combination and political agitation. As the *Hindoo Patriot* of Harish Chandra Mukherjee wrote in clear terms: “Our countrymen have learnt that if India is ever to improve in her political condition, it will not indeed by the force of arms but by the united will and inflexible determination of her sons never to yield their lawful rights to the voracious rapacity and insolent hauteur of any class of oppressors”.

Chapter 3

Educated Indians

Many of the educated Indians who had supported the indigo cultivators against the tyranny of the European planters were themselves a disillusioned lot. They had acquired qualifications in new education only to find that these were not suitable for any employment outside the public establishments. Yet the number of aspirants for such qualifications had been on the increase since a knowledge in the English language had been declared useful for a lower level job in a British establishment. In 1835 English had replaced Persian as the official language and in 1857 when the revolt of the sepoys was in progress, three universities were set up on London model at the three metropolitan cities of British India—— Calcutta, Bombay and Madras. By 1873, the number of successful candidates from Matriculation onwards was 12,392 at Calcutta, 5,502 at Madras and 2,703 at Bombay. Having received a good secondary school education up to the Matriculation level and having attended a university, these youngmen were educated and compared to the illiterate town-dwellers and village ryots, very well-educated indeed.

What was the prospect open to the large number of students who were thus able to receive higher education in the country? For one thing the career in India was never virtually open to talent though the principle had been asserted time and again in the Charter Act of 1833 and the Queen's Proclamation of 1858 as we have already seen, to allay fear, suspicion and distrust after the outbreak. Again some avenues like army and police were closed altogether. In those days agriculture offered little temptation and so did manufacturing and commerce for the latter was almost impossible without skill, capital and equality of terms with which it could compete with European industry. As a matter of fact, the very nature of the courses with their unique and disproportionate attention to literature and philosophy, compared with physical and cognate branches of practical instruction, tended to limit the choice of a career to either government service or analogous employment.

In theory the Covenanted Civil Service was open to the educated Indians since 1853 but in practice every difficulty stood in their way— the very early age-limits for the examination, the nature of the syllabus, the expense of going to London where the examination was held, the prejudice against crossing the "blackwater", and the official reluctance to admit Indians into this vital service. Only posts at the lower level of the Uncovenanted Civil Service were open to the Indians. Here the salaries were very poor, prospects for promotions nil and service conditions extremely bad. Since men were not often employed outside their own provinces, less than two thousand jobs were available in the Uncovenanted Executive and Judicial Branches in Bengal, Bombay and Madras. Not all of them were given to the educated: in Bombay and in Madras less than half of the Uncovenanted Civilians had qualifications in the new education while in the North Western Provinces and in the Punjab most of these posts went to those who could not boast of any qualifications at all.

The non-availability of suitable opening in the public service naturally compelled many to turn to independent professions such as teaching, law, journalism and medicine. Unlike the government servants who were cramped by dependence on the good will of their employers, here they had greater incentive for taking part in public life. By the end of 1870s, there was hardly any important town in British India which did not possess a sprinkle of teachers, lawyers, journalists and doctors who took a very lively and keen interest in social, political, economical and religious questions of the day, thanks to the massive expansion of the press, both Indian and English, that had taken place in the last few decades of the nineteenth century.

It was this group of professionals who unmasked the British rule in India. They explained how Britain was developing India as a colony to further her own material prosperity. In the process India had become a supplier of raw materials to Britain, a market for British manufacturers, and a field for investment of British capital. India's development was retarded at a time when most of the countries in Europe were fast becoming developed countries in the world. Foremost among these persons was Dadabhai Naoroji who pointed out that the poverty of the Indian people was not inherent in the Indian conditions but was caused by the huge drain of wealth from India which, besides providing employment to thousands of Englishmen and supporting British mercantile interests in India, maintained an army to further British interests in the countries neighbouring India. The plight of the educated but unemployed youngmen in the post-1857 years stirred his heart: "The thousands that are being sent out by the universities every year find themselves in a most anomalous position. They may beg in the streets, or break stones in roads. They may perish or do what they like or can, but scores of Europeans must go from this country [England] to take up what belongs to them, and that in spite of every profession for years and years past of English statesmen, that they must govern India for India's good, by solemn Acts and declarations of Parliament and above all, by the words of the august Sovereign herself."

Chapter 4

Political Associations

The revelation of the true nature of the British Raj in India in the post-1857 years galvanised the educated Indians into highlighting it through forming political associations—many of them with newspapers and periodicals as organs of their nationalist activities. Such associations did exist before 1857—in 1837 the Zamindary Association, later renamed as the Landholders' Society was formed in Bengal and in 1843 Bengal British Indian Society came into existence. In the wake of 'the Black Acts" controversy of 1849 which emanated out of the four bills introduced by Bethune, the Law Member of the Governor-General's Council, to do away with the privilege of the British-born subjects of trial by the Calcutta Supreme Court alone, the foundation of the British Indian Association was laid at Calcutta on 31 October 1851 when the Landholders' Society of 1837 merged with the Bengal British Indian Society of 1843 to give birth to a stronger political body. This was followed by the foundation of the Bombay Association and the Madras Native Association in 1852. At the time of the renewal of the Charter Act of the East India Company in 1853, British Indian Association submitted a petition to the British Parliament with a list of demands which included, among others, reduction of postage for newspapers, relaxation of the pressure of the revenue system, improvement of judicial administration, protection of the life and property of the people from molestation, encouragement to indigenous manufacturers, education of the people, admission of Indians to higher administrative posts and finally enlargement of the Governor-General's Legislative Council with admission of some Indian members. It may be mentioned here that Rammohun Roy who is regarded as "the father of political regeneration in India" submitted a similar petition some twenty years ago on a similar occasion in 1833 including many of the demands of the British Indian Association.

However, with the transfer of the power from the Company to the Crown and the start of a reactionary policy by the British Raj, these associations, local in nature and dominated by upper classes who were often very loyal to the administration for their prosperity, seemed to have outlived their utility in the changed circumstances. In the pre-1857 years when education was the monopoly of the few well placed persons, British connextion was seen by the educated Indians as a step towards the transformation of medieval India into a modern India. This explained the loyalty of the educated classes to the British Raj when it was shaken by the outbreak in 1857. In the post-1857 years this illusion gradually disappeared as the successive pledges of justice and fair play made in the Charter Acts of 1833 and 1853 and the Queen's Proclamation of 1858 were scarcely implemented and a bleak and gloomy prospect stared in the face of the educated Indians. It was necessary now to agitate for political reforms by creating a public opinion for them, not only in India but also in England, the home of the British Raj. With that end in view, three societies in quick succession were founded in London—the East Indian Association of Dadabhai Naoroji in 1866, the National Indian Association of Mary Carpenter in 1867 and the Indian Society of Ananda Mohan Bose in 1872. These organisations which included many liberal minded Englishmen did useful work for the cause of reforms in India. In India in 1867 the Poona Sarvajanik Sabha was organised by M.G. Ranade, G.K. Gokhale, G.V. Joshi, S.H. Chiplunkar and G.N. Deshpande and in Calcutta in 1875 was started India League to stimulate the sense of nationalism amongst the people and awaken political consciousness among them.

However, the organisation which played a prominent role in rousing the political consciousness of the Indian people in the pre-Congress years was the one born at Calcutta one year after the Indian League and the circumstances leading to its birth may be briefly noted here. In 1869 Surendra Nath Banerjea was one of the three Indians who passed the Covenanted Civil Service examination successfully but was dismissed from the service within a few years on trivial grounds. In 1875 Banerjea went to England to appeal to the Secretary of State but his appeal fell on deaf ears. He also found the doors to the Bar closed and returned to India as a disillusioned youngman. Banerjea later wrote in his book, *A Nation in Making,* that his case illustrated "the helpless impotency of our people" and he decided to address himself to the task of helping "our helpless people in the direction of redressing our wrongs and protecting our rights, both as individuals and as a nation." He keenly felt the need for an all-India body for the purpose and in collaboration with Ananda Mohan Bose, he formed an association which was inaugurated at a very largely attended meeting at the Albert Hall in Calcutta on 26 July 1876. It was named "the Indian Association" with its object such as those which included promotion "by every legitimate means, the political, intellectual, and national advancement of the people." At the inaugural meeting at the Albert Hall, Banerjea justified the creation of yet another association at Calcutta besides the British Indian Association and the Indian League by pointing out that none of these associations represented "the oppressed cooly or the oppressed ryot" or possessed an organisation "capable of keeping up and stimulating public opinion." The Indian Association was to represent all classes of the Indian people and was to be "the centre of an all-India movement" based on "the conception of a united India, derived from the inspiration of Mazzin," of the Italian Unification fame.

Chapter 5

Civil Service

Immediately after the birth of the Indian Association, Surendra Nath Banerjea's finest hour for organising an all-India movement came when in 1876 the maximum age-limit for the Civil Service examination was reduced from twenty-one to nineteen by Salisbury, the Secretary of State for India. This created a painful impression throughout India, and was regarded as a deliberate attempt to blast the prospects of Indian candidates for the Indian Civil Service. Indeed, educated Indians felt very strongly about the Civil Service question because with it were associated not only their ambitions for power and position but also their dreams of ultimate self-government. Both Bose and Banerjea of the Indian Association felt that the issue of lowering the maximum age-limit by two years was "indeed a national question" which called for "a national movement." They decided to organize a national protest against this reduction invoking the Charter Act of 1833 and the Queen's Proclamation of 1858 where the rights of the Indian, irrespective of class, creed and colour, for service in the administration had been acknowledged.

On 24 March 1877 a public meeting was held at the Albert Hall, Calcutta and a committee consisting of the representatives of all sections of the Indian community in Calcutta was appointed to draw up a memorial drawing attention to the principles and pledges contained in the Charter Act of 1833 and the Queen's

Proclamation of 1858 and demanding not only the restoration of the higher age-limit but also the holding of the examination simultaneously in India and in England. In the summer of 1877 Banerjea led a whirlwind campaign in Northern India, holding meetings at Agra, Lahore, Amritsar, Meerut, Allahabad, Delhi, Cawnpore, Lucknow, Aligarh, Benares and Patna and in the following winter visited Bombay, Ahmedabad, Surat, Poona and Madras to mobilize support in favour of the memorial. And in April 1879 Lal Mohan Ghosh was sent to England to present it in person as the representative of the Indian Association.

The Civil Service agitation of 1877-79 which received the warmest support from the educated Indians throughout India was organised and co-ordinated with such extreme care and constitutional manner that it drew admiration from the Europeans also. "The really remarkable feature of the whole movement", wrote the *Times of India* on 24 December 1877 "is the moderation, the good sense, and political tact which have distinguished it from first to last. A race that can conduct a political campaign with such ability has already won half the battle". Banerjea's "triumphal progress" through various parts of India and his stirring speeches established his reputation as a national leader. Unlike Keshab Chandra Sen of the Brahma Samaj and Dayanand Saraswati of the Arya Smaj who had already toured the subcontinent in order to propagate their religions views following a very ancient tradition, Banerjea was the first Indian to do so on a purely political mission. There is no doubt that his mission brought about a union among educated men of diverse castes, creeds, classes and regions in the country and effectively demonstrated that "the people of India could combine and unite for the attainment of their common political ends". The contacts thus forged by Banerjea's mission with different parts of the British India could now be effectively used for future agitational purposes.

Chapter 6

Vernacular Press Act

An occasion to test the political contacts formed by Banerjea during the course of the Civil Service agitation in 1877 soon occurred when Lytton passed the Vernacular Press Act in 1878. By that year there were about 400 Indian-owned newspapers, the majority of which were in the vernaculars. There can be no doubt that some of the Indian newspapers were becoming increasingly hostile to the British Raj. Their principal topics of discussion were the injustice and tyranny of the Raj, its utter want of consideration towards its subjects, the insolence and pride of Britons in India, the drain of wealth from the country and the growing pauperization of the people, the exclusion of Indians from higher jobs in the army and the civil services, the partiality and preference shown for Britons in employment and the administration of justice, over-taxation and over-legislation, the denial of any voice to Indians in the government of their own country, and the attempts of the British Government to emasculate the Indian people materially and morally. Moreover, these newspapers had now begun to debate, openly or covertly, the desirability of gaining independence from British rule and how best it could be achieved. In November 1874, a Bombay civilian, F.P. Lely, published a long article on the vernacular press in the *Indian Economist* of Calcutta and with the help of extracts culled from the official weekly reports on Indian newspapers, Lely proved that the tone of the vernacular press, particularly in Bengal and Bombay, was extremely seditious and unless something was done to alter it or to neutralize its effects, "we may as well give up all hope of basing our Empire on the good will of the people and trust to our guns alone." In April 1876, Lytton, Salisbury's nominee succeeded Northbrook as the Viceroy and he immediately addressed himself to the task of imposing restrictions on the freedom of the vernacular press but encountered stiff opposition from the Law Member of his Council, Arthur Hobhouse. After Hobhouse had left India, Lytton wrote a confidential minute on 22 October 1877, emphasising the urgent need to stop seditious writing in the Indian press. Having obtained the assent of all local governments except Madras, Lytton passed the very stringent gagging Bill at a single sitting of the Legislative Council on 14 March 1878, without giving either the Indian people or the Council of the Secretary of State, a chance to consider it. The Vernacular Press Act authorized magistrates, with the previous sanction of local governments, to demand bonds from printers and publishers and either a deposit of such sum as the local government might think fit or the submission of proofs for inspection. If any newspaper published any objectionable materials, it would be warned first and if this warning were disregarded, the machinery and copies of the newspaper could be confiscated. The only appeal against this was to the Governor-General-in-Council. A Press Commissioner was appointed whose real function was to manage the press.

As in the case of the Civil Service agitation, it was the Indian Association of Calcutta which took the lead in organising the protest against the Act after obtaining messages from several political associations in different parts of the country. The Act had been universally condemned by the Native Press Association formed in December 1876 at Delhi on the occasion of the Imperial Darbar and by the great Liberal leader, W.E. Gladstone and several prominent journalists and politicians in Britain. On 17 April 1878 the Indian Association held a meeting at Calcutta which was attended by about 4,000 people, mostly students, passed a resolution on the freedom of the press and drafted a memorial against the Act which was forwarded to Gladstone who presented it to Parliament along with similar other memorials received from Bombay and Poona. On 23 July 1878 in an important debate on the subject in the House of Commons Gladstone exposed the hollowness of the case for muzzling the vernacular press in India and attacked the sudden and secret manner in which the Act had been passed. The opposition to the Act was defeated but there was clear indication that the Act could not remain for long in the Statute Book after the Liberals had come to power. At the moment however, the Act indirectly encouraged the growth of Indian-owned English newspapers–the *Hindu* at Madras and the *Deccan Star* at Poona which later merged with the *Mahratta*, while the *Amrita Bazar Patrika* of Calcutta, "the most subtle and ingeniously exasperating of Bengali organs, transformed itself between two issues from a bilingual to an English journal, and thus slipped, with derisive chuckles, out of the grasp of Sir Ashley Eden", the Lt. Governor of Bengal.

Despite the failure of the movement against the Vernacular Press Act to achieve its immediate objects, the movement was significant in more than one way in the history of the freedom movement in India. First, Gladstone's speech against the Vernacular Press Act in the House of Commons revived the Indian nationalist's drooping faith in Britain, the British Parliament and the British Liberals. The Indian Association thanked Gladstone and other M.Ps like Bright, Morley and Ripon who had supported the cause of the Vernacular Press in India at a special meeting at Calcutta on 6 September 1878. Secondly, the Vernacular Press Act now drew India, hitherto treated above party politics, into the vortex of party strife in Britain, affecting the Britons in India also. As the speeches and writings of the Liberals in Britain became increasingly critical of the Tory policies in India, the hearts of the Indian nationalists began to be filled with joy and hope. Thirdly, the agitation against the Vernacular Press Act marked the transfer of leadership from the wealthy upper class to the educated middle class represented mostly by students who had been organised into "unions" particularly in Calcutta and elsewhere in Bengal, by Banerjea and Bose. Obviously the wealthy upper class had more interests at stake in the Civil Service agitation last year than in the agitation for the repeal of the Vernacular Press Act. At the meeting of 17 April in Calcutta, Rashbehari Ghosh regretted "the absence of Maharajas, and Rajas, of Nawabs and Khan Bahadurs" and commented that after all, they were only the "Corinthian capitals of society" and did not constitute the structure itself despite adding "grace and beauty" to it. And finally, the Vernacular Press Act brought the press and political associations into closer contact with each other than before. The links between the two were already there as we have already said that many of the political associations had their own press organs and the conductors of their press were often active members of political associations. Yet, before the Vernacular Press Act it was the political associations which had needed the press more than the press had needed them. However, when the press in India was put into fetters in 1878, it was the political associations of Calcutta and Poona which came to its rescue. The lesson of inter-dependence thus learnt was not lost on the Indian press, which now began to preach the value of more effective political organization with far greater zeal than before.

Chapter 7

White Munity

Hopes raised by the Liberal's support for the agitation against the Vernacular Press Act in the hearts of the Indian nationalists were kindled further when the Liberals were returned to power in Great Britain in the spring of 1880. Lytton resigned and in his place Ripon, a former member of the Indian Reform Society in London, was appointed Viceroy in June 1880. Gladstone considered it to be "our weakness and our calamity" that "we have not been able to give to India the benefits and blessings of free institutions". Ripon set out with the intention of making a beginning in that direction. In January 1882 he repealed Lytton's infamous Vernacular Press Act and within five months on 18 May 1882 announced his resolution on local self-government which was desirable not so much as "an improvement in administration" but "as a measure of political and popular education."

Ripon favoured the creation of local boards, both municipal and rural, with jurisdiction over areas sufficiently small to ensure that all their members had an interest in, and knowledge of, their affairs. The boards should contain at least a two-thirds majority of elected non-official members, and be presided over by a non-official chairman and should have definite and adequate funds at their disposal. Government control should be exercised from without rather than from within and the boards should have freedom of initiative and real power and responsibilities. However, Ripon soon realized by the autumn of 1882 that his local self-government scheme which had inspired the Indians could not be speedily and fully implemented because of the opposition of most British officials in India and members of the India Council in London. He therefore requested Allan Octavian Hume, a British civilian who had retired from the service in January 1882, had been living in Simla since then and enjoyed the trust and affection of the Indians, to tell the Indians about the difficulties he was experiencing and that they should not add to his difficulties by giving way to impatience or cynicism.

Ripon's attempt to "put the native on the gadi" as his local self-government scheme was cynically described by those opposed to it widened the gulf between him and the British officials and commercial Europeans in India. It was in this circumstance when Ilbert, the Law Member of Ripon's Council, sought to withdraw the privilege, hitherto enjoyed by European British subjects in the districts, of trial by a judge of their own race and to enable Indian sessions judges to try them in a bill on 2 February 1883, it was the signal for them to revolt.

In Calcutta, a small group of Europeans from the local bar, press and Chamber of Commerce took the lead in organizing the movement against the Ilbert Bill. It got in touch with the Europeans all over India and influential persons in Britain and persuaded Ripon to postpone a discussion on the Bill from 23 February to 9 March to gain sufficient time to organize a widespread agitation against it. At an angry and crowded meeting of Europeans and Eurasians held in Calcutta on 28 February, speakers vied with one another in denouncing the Bill and in abusing Indians to the evident delight of their audience. "No such excitement has been witnessed among the Europeans since the time of the Munity," the top people at home was informed by the Calcutta correspondent of *The Times*. Committees to raise funds and memorialize the authorities in India and Britain against the Bill were organised in all important towns in India and on 29 March the Committee to conduct and coordinate the agitation flowered into an European and Anglo-Indian Defence Association. The prospectus of the Association referred to the "rapid increase in the numbers and importance of the European community" in India in recent years and stressed the urgent need to counter "the extra-ordinary development amongst the natives of associations having a political object" and "the tendency of much recent legislation and administrative action to disregard the interests of the European community."

For nine months the Defence Association carried on a ceaseless and virulent campaign against the Ilbert Bill. Embarrassed by the agitation, the British Government asked Ripon to reach a speedy settlement of the vexed questions. The threat of a renewed vulgar European demonstration in Calcutta leading to a possible riot and collision with Indians who had started organising meetings and memorials in support of the Ilbert Bill, and the probability of continued European opposition to the operation of the Bill when passed, made most members of Ripon's Executive Council advocate a policy of appeasement of the agitators. The government now modified the Bill to such an extent as to give the European offenders the right of claiming even in the most trivial cases, trial by jury, of which at least half the members must be Europeans.

The success of the anti-Ilbert Bill agitation "left a rankling sense of humiliation in the mind of educated India" but it also taught them the value of combination and organisation. As George Campbell, speaking in the House of Commons on 23 August 1883, urged the British Government not to withdraw the Bill since it would be "an enormous evil" to yield to the European agitation against the Bill "on account of the example it would give the Natives of the advantage and power of agitation". The immediate events of the year after August 1883 proved Campbell as a prophetic observer. As before, Banerjea took the lead in organisation.

Chapter 8

National Conference

When feeling were running high on the Ilbert Bill question, Surendra Nath Banerjea was prosecuted on a contempt of court for writing an article in the *Bengalee* on 2 April 1883, criticising the high-handed and arrogant behaviour of a "young and raw" judge of the Calcutta High Court, J.F. Norris. On 5 May when the case came up for hearing before a full bench of the Calcutta High Court, Banerjea apologized and withdrew his remarks at the advice of his counsel, W.C. Bonnerjee but the court sentenced him to two months' imprisonment. A section of the vast crowd, consisting mostly of students, greeted the sentence by smashing the windows of the courtroom and pelting the police with stones and the Indian part of Calcutta observed a hartal.

The news of the imprisonment of Banerjea who had become the idol of young educated Indians spread like wildfire and led to demonstrations all over India. The demonstrations were joined by people of all ages, classes and creeds. Writing about this fact, the editor of the *Englishman* remarked that it showed "the existence of a common motive, political rather than religious, to which all natives irrespective of creed, are ready to respond".

After his release from prison, a largely attended public meeting at Calcutta on 17 July 1883 resolved to raise a National Fund, the idea of which had recently become very popular, to secure the political advancement of the country by means of constitutional agitation in India and England and that the other provinces be invited to join in the movement. A sum of Rs. 20,000 was collected and handed over to the Indian Association for the purpose. It was however felt that the administration of a national fund needed a truly national organisation and the Indian Association did not answer that description though as early as 27 May 1882 in the wake of the publication of Ripon's resolution on local self-government Banerjea had announced in the *Bengalee* the idea of organizing such an association, "National Congress" annually by the Indian Association next year. The feelings evoked by his imprisonment and the Ilbert Bill question seemed to favour formation of such a national organisation now and the necessary opportunity was provided by the proposal of the Government of India to hold an International Exhibition in Calcutta in December 1883 when many persons from the different parts of India would be around. Backed by the support of all the branches of the Indian Association in North India as well as of the leading political associations of Bombay and Madras, the first National Conference was held in Calcutta on 28, 29 and 30 December 1883.

The proceedings began with a national hymn when at midday on 28 December about one hundred persons from various parts of the country assembled at the Albert Hall, Calcutta. Ramtanu Lahiri was elected Chairman and A.M. Bose formally opened the Conference which he described in his welcome address as "the first session of the Indian Parliament" and emphasised the need for holding similar conferences in the future. On 29 December the Conference adopted a resolution on simultaneous holding of the Civil Service examination in Britain and India and raising the upper age-limit for it to twenty-two and prescribing an intellectual test for appointments to the Statutory Civil Service for the princes. The separation of the judiciary from the executive also figured in the subjects of discussion on the second day and on the last day the Conference passed four resolutions: the first emphasized the value of raising a national fund, the second stressed the need of establishing representative assemblies in India, the third demanded the repeal of the Arms Act which prohibited Indians from carrying any arms and the fourth expressed "deep regret" at the recent "concordat" over the Ilbert Bill. Thus educated Indian belonging to various classes and creeds from more than forty-five different places in the country met and discussed many questions of national interest at a national conference despite the absence of any representatives from the British Indian Association and the two Muslim organizations in Calcutta. The National Conference symbolised the desire of the educated Indians for a national political organisation in India–a desire that was growing stronger every year.

The Second session of the National Conference was also held in Calcutta in 1885 on 25, 26, and 27 December. Representatives from more than thirty political associations all over India including the British Indian Association attended it this time and resolved to hold the meeting every year at important places like Bombay, Madras and Allahabad. At the conclusion of the National Conference on 27 December 1885, a telegram was dispatched to another national conference meeting at another place far away from Calcutta: "The delegates in Conference assembled in Calcutta desire to express their deep sympathy with the approaching conference in Bombay." It was the National Congress about to hold its first session in Bombay under the presidency of W.C. Bonnerjee.

Chapter 9

National Congress

Despite the fact that the emergence of a national organization like the Indian Congress was only a question of time, the part played by Allan Octavian Hume, who was free from any regional loyalties, in hastening its birth by December 1885 can not be underestimated. Son of Joseph Hume, the founder of the Radical Party in England, Hume retired early from the Civil Service in January 1882 and was living in Simla when the publication of the scheme for local self-government in India drew him closer to Ripon. His friendship with the educated Indians led Ripon to use him as a rapporteur between the Viceroy and the educated Indians and the test case was provided when his local self-government scheme was provoking bitter opposition from the Europeans in India much to the annoyance of the educated Indians, as we have already seen.

When the agitation against the Ilbert Bill was started by the Europeans in India, Hume realized that Indians, particularly those in Bengal which housed the head quarters of the British Raj, needed to organize themselves not only in self-defence but also in order to strengthen the hands of the Viceroy who was the principal target of the European fury. On 1 March 1883, the day after the notorious Calcutta meeting where Indians were virulently abused by Europeans, he wrote a long letter, presumably private and confidential, addressed to the graduates of the Calcutta University, in which he made an earnest and sincere appeal to their sense of patriotism and public spirit and advised them to organize themselves into a compact and disciplined body with the object of promoting the mental, moral, social and political regeneration of their country. Hume proposed that a beginning might be made with a body of fifty "founders" who would finalize the details of the organization. He, however, suggested as to the personnel, discipline and working methods of the proposed association, laying special emphasis on its constitution being democratic and its members being free from personal ambition.

Hume's letter had two immediate gains–the first was a joint memorial submitted to the Viceroy on 8 March 1883, thanking him for the Ilbert Bill, by six leading associations of Calcutta until recently at loggerheads with each other. They were the British Indian Association, the Mohammedan Literary Society, the National Mahomedan Association, the East Bengal Association, the Indian Association, and the Vakil's Association. The second was the formation at Calcutta in April 1883 of a body called "the United Indian Committee" to apprise the people of Great Britain of the views and sentiments of the people of India in regard to all matters of administration and legislation relating to India, "with special reference to the Bill now before the Imperial Legislative Council of India for the amendment of the Code of Criminal Procedure". The President of the United Indian Committee was W.C. Bonnerjee, a close friend of Hume. In May 1883 the Committee sent Lal Mohan Ghosh to Britain to counter the propaganda of the agents of the European and Anglo Indian Defence Association. However, this fact and the existence of the Committee itself was not known to many till the disclosure made by the *Bangabasi* on 17 November 1883. In March next year the Committee blossomed into the Indian Union with the Maharaja of Darbhanga as its President and W.C. Bonnerjee as its Secretary. It was intended to be a sort of Indian Defence Association representing the whole nation and acting in concert with the other public bodies.

In the second half of 1884 when Ripon was preparing to retire from India in December 1884, as desired by the British Cabinet which had selected Dufferin as his successor, Hume was busy consolidating the network of his contacts all over India and transforming it into the nucleus of a "national party." On 16 November 1884, he wrote to S.H. Chiplunkar, the Secretary of the Poona Sarvajanik Sabha, regarded by Hume "as the leading sabha" in India: "I may tell you in strict confidence that Lord Ripon has made a point of my coming down to meet him at Bombay. Tho' he knows Lord Dufferin well and tho' the latter's letters to him since his appointment seem to promise well for the National Cause yet we cannot feel any surety as to the line he is likely to pursue until Lord Ripon has thoroughly discussed the situation with him. This he will do at Calcutta and he will then communicate the results to me at Bombay. I propose to make a little private tour–having made the personal acquaintance of all the earnest men in Bombay and having discussed the situation with them–I propose to come on to Poona and do the same to you. Then go on to Madras, Calcutta, Patna (perhaps Dacca), Benares, Allahabad, Agra, Delhi, Amritsar and Lahore–possibly also Lucknow and some other places. I want to make a practical effort towards that "linking in" which has now become a matter of vital importance to us."

In December 1884 Hume came to Bombay to bid farewell to Ripon and utilized his stay there till the end of February next year in discussing with the Bombay leaders these subjects: the organization of a central "national association" to direct political activity throughout the country; the holding of an annual conference of representative men from all parts of India; the preparation of a chapter of Indian demands for presentation to the British Parliament; the establishment of a "telegraphic agency" to present Indian views to the British press as well as to counter the misrepresentations of Europeans including those of the Calcutta correspondent of the *Times* and finally the formation of an "Indian

Party" in the British Parliament. In Bombay Hume was also joined by the Poona Sarvajanik Sabha leaders who might have been persuaded by him to agree to his suggestion to play host to the first "Conference of the Indian National Union" to be held in December 1885. Before Hume left for Madras in early March, the "legal trio", Mehta, Telang and Tyabji, launched the Bombay Presidency Association to fulfill the long felt need of educated men of Bombay to have a political association of their own. After visiting Madras where he discussed privately with local leaders the political programme he had already matured in Bombay, Hume came to Calcutta on 19 March and stayed there with Manmohan Ghosh and discussed with W.C. Bonnerjee and N.N. Sen the proposed conference of the Indian National Union. It must be mentioned here that Hume did not meet to discuss anything with Surendra Nath Banerjea who was not considered to be a member of his "inner circle." On his way back to Simla from Calcutta in April, Hume visited several places in the North Western Provinces and the Punjab.

Back in Simla in May 1885, Hume consulted Dufferin who warmly approved his proposal of the conference in Poona in December 1885 as it would furnish the government with the views and wishes of the educated Indians throughout the country. However he threw cold water on Hume's suggestion to invite Lord Reay, Governor of Bombay, to be the first President: "Don't ask Lord Reay to preside –don't have officials–if you gentlemen do your duty, you will criticize the administration and officials ought not to take part in this." When Hume agreed with Dufferin, the latter wished him "every success." It was only after his meeting with Dufferin that Hume issued a private and confidential circular among the members of "the inner circle of the National Party" about the "Conference of the National Union" to be held at Poona from "the 25th to 31st of December 1885." These dates later clashed with those of the National Conference at Calcutta when in November 1885 Surendra Nath Banerjea issued a circular on holding the meeting on 25, 26, and 27 December 1885. On Hume's return to Bombay on 2 December 1885 from a visit of England starting on 14 July, the embarrassed leaders of the Poona Sarvajanik Sabha and the Bombay President Association, after a hurried consultations, decided to call their forthcoming "Conference" at Poona "Congress" so as to avoid confusion with the proposed "National Conference" at Calcutta and also to postpone the start of their meeting from 25 to 28 December, a day after the Calcutta Conference was over.

The first public announcement of the forthcoming Congress was made by the Madras tri-weekly, *Hindu*, on 5 December and when the Poona Sarvajanik Sabha had completed all the necessary arrangement, an outbreak of cholera in the town forced the organizers to shift the venue to Bombay in the third week of December. Thanks to the Bombay Presidency Association, all necessary arrangements were ready by the morning of 27 December when the delegates to the Congress began to arrive.

At midday, on 28 December, Monday, the first meeting of the Indian National Congress began in the hall of the Gokuldas Tejpal Sanskrit College with 72 delegates, mostly lawyers, journalists and teachers, who had elected themselves by paying a small fee. Hume's proposal that W.C. Bonnerjee should be elected President of the Congress, was seconded by S. Subramanian Aiyar and supported by Telang and carried unanimously. The election of Bonnerjee, while assuaging any soreness that the people of Bengal might have felt on account of the manner in which the Congress was convened, established a healthy precedent of choosing the President of the Congress from a province other than the one in which the Congress was being held.

In his presidential address to the Congress delegates, Bonnerjee outlined the following objects for the Indian National Congress:

"(a) The promotion of personal intimacy and friendship amongst all the more earnest workers in our country's cause in [all] part of the Empire.

(b) The eradication by direct friendly intercourse of all possible race, creed, or provincial prejudices amongst all lovers of our country, and the fuller development and consolidation of those sentiments of national unity that had their origin in their beloved Lord Ripon's ever memorable reign.

(c) The authoritative record, after this has been carefully elicited by the fullest discussion, of the matured opinions of the educated classes in India on some of the more important and pressing of the [political and] social questions of the day.

(d) The determination of the lines upon the methods by which during the next twelve months it is desirable for native politicians to labour in the public interests."

The moderate tone of the Congress for the next few years atleast was set by Bonnerjee, a fully Anglicised educated Indian, when he refuted in advance that the Congress was "a nest of conspirators and disloyalists." He affirmed that there were no more thoroughly loyal and consistent well-wishers of the British Government than were himself and the friends around them. He asserted that India was "truly grateful" to Great Britain for all that had been done for "the benefit of India" though much "remained to be done." For example, "the basis of the government should be widened and the people should have their proper and legitimate share in it" and this was "in no way incompatible with their thorough loyalty to the British Government." In meeting to discuss in an orderly and peaceable manner questions of vital importance affecting their well-being, they were following the only course which the constitution of England enabled them to represent their views to the ruling authority. Those who spoke at the first session of the Indian National Congress–Sen from Bengal, Mehta, Telang and Naoroji from Bombay, Murlidhar from Ambala, Ghosh from Allahabad and Aiyar from Madras–displayed similar moderation and felt that the Congress was creating history as a symbol and vindication of their growing unity as a nation.

For four days the Congress discussed and passed altogether nine resolutions. Among them six were demands made to the British Raj for the (a) appointment of a Royal Commission of Enquiry into the working of the British administration in India; (b) abolition of the India Council of the Secretary of State in London; (c) creation of Legislative Councils in the North Western Provinces and the Punjab; (d) admission of elected members in the Legislative Council with the right of interpellation and discussion of budgets, and the creation of a standing committee in the House of Commons to consider formal protests from majorities in the Councils; (e) reduction of military expenditure and its equitable apportionment between India and England and finally introduction of simultaneous Civil Service examinations in England and India and the raising of the age of candidates. Discussion of the burning social problems of the day seems to have been excluded from the agenda to add force to the political nature of the organisation. Yet there were many at the first session for whom reform of the society was very dear to their hearts and they held informal discussions on the subject.

Thus was born in 1885 the political giant of the twentieth century, symbolizing the birth of a new India and a new nation. As *Indu Prakash* wrote on the opening day of the Congress: "The very fact that such a Conference has met and fairly promises to be a success belies the supposition that we are not a nation. It must be conceded that we are wanting in many qualities which make a nation. We are divided by a variety of languages, religions, and social customs, separated from each other by long distances, and are wanting in homogeneity of race and feeling. Nevertheless it is undeniable that we are at present politically one nation, or at least have the markings of one." Had the successive Viceroys responded favourably to the demands made by the educated Indians on the platform of the Indian National Congress annually since 1885, the Congress would have perhaps remained for many years a "safety-valve" as Hume described it. The failure of the British Raj to do so was to transform the "safety-valve" into a "time-bomb" for British imperialism in India in a none too distant future.

Section II

The Years of the Moderate Congress and the Extremist Challenge, 1885-1918

Chapter 10

Moderate Phase till 1892

The nine resolutions passed by the Indian National Congress were widely circulated and discussed by the local political associations. The National Conference of Surendra Nath Banerjea which had met earlier at Calcutta in December 1885 found that the resolutions of the Congress almost fully reflected its views. And Banerjea wondered about the justification of continuing its seperate identity. The Congress sponsored by a well-known retired British civilian and started with the blessings of the British Viceroy Dufferin, stood more chances of commanding both respect and success as a national organisation in India. So at the next meeting of the Congress in Calcutta in December 1886 under the presidency of Dadabhai Naoroji, the National Conference of Banerjea silently merged with it and from that date Banerjea took an active interest in the Congress Movement and became one of the strongest pillars of the Congress organisation like Naoroji, Mehta and Tyabji.

The number of delegates to the Congress session in Calcutta increased to 440 and though the National Muhammedan Association held aloof, the British Indian Association joined the session for the first time. A Bengali tone and character was added to the Congress in Calcutta which was the seat of the Viceroys, to such an extent that Dufferin wrote to Cross, the Secretary of State, in January 1887 after the Congress session had been over that the Indian National Congress was a "Bangalee Constitution". The third session of the Congress held in Madras in December 1887 was presided over by Badruddin Tyabji, who later became a judge of the Bombay High Court. This time the number of delegates rose to 607 and the need was felt to draft a constitution for it and a committee of 34 members was set up for the purpose. Another important development at the Madras Congress was the emergence of the Subjects Committee. In the first two Congresses the task of preparing drafts of resolutions which were to be moved at the public session was left to a few senior delegates. This was violently opposed by the younger section of the delegates and it was decided to set up at the opening of each session of the Congress a small representative committee to fix up the programme and prepare the drafts of the resolution for the open session. The Subjects Committee which henceforth became a regular feature of the Congress Movement made the first breach in the strong citadel of conservative leadership of the Congress.

The Congress at Calcutta and Madras passed a series of resolutions which were almost a clear repetition of those passed at the inaugural Congress at Bombay, to "instruct the Government." However, the resolutions fell on the deaf ears of "the Government" and "the Government" refused "to be instructed." Disappointed with the attitude of the Government of India, Hume, the guiding spirit of the Congress, decided to bring pressure upon it by widening the base of the Congress Movement. As a first step, he decided to organise public opinion in its favour both in India and England. Apart from organization of meetings in India, a paid agency was established in London in 1888 to educate public opinion in England by arranging lectures and distributing pamphlets. It was later replaced by the British Committee of the Congress which published a weekly, *India.* In India Hume organised numerous public meetings which were quite well-attended. He also wrote and distributed many pamphlets, two of which entitled, "A Conversation between Maulvi Furreduddin and one Ram Buksh of Kambakhatpur" created great stir by depicting the evils of the British land revenue system and the despotic nature of the British

Government in India. The pamphlets suggested that it was only the representative government which could remedy these evils and since Congress was fighting for this type of government, people in large number should join it now.

Such an attempt at organising a mass movement was certain to harden the official attitude to the Congress which was hitherto not inhospitable—Dufferin had invited the Congress delegates to a garden party at its Calcutta session in December 1886 and the next year in December 1887 when the Congress held its session in Madras, the Madras Governor had followed Dufferin's example. Dufferin now publicly declared at St. Andrew's Dinner in Calcutta in 1887 the Congress to be a "Microscopic minority"—an organisation which consisted of a few urban educated elites only and did not represent the masses. The officials took the cue from Dufferin's judgement on the Congress. Besides a suggestion to deport Hume, the officials laboured hard to frustrate the holding of the December 1888 session at Allahabad. They also encouraged, Syed Ahmad Khan, the founder of the Muhammedan Anglo-Oriental College at Aligarh in 1875 to set up with the support of a loyal Hindu Zamindar, Raja Shiva Prasad, United Indian Patriotic Association in 1888 as a parallel to the Congress Movement. Syed Ahmad Khan who had been a supporter of Hindu-Muslim unity earlier dramatically changed after the Congress had held its first session at Bombay in December 1885. He reacted to the Congress Movement by organising an Educational Congress in 1886 as he felt that the Muslims would not benefit by joining it and education was all that they needed at the moment to ensure their progress. Since the Calcutta Congress he had been openly asking the Muslims not to join the Congress Movement. Inspite of Syed Ahmad Khan's hostility which was now backed by the British Raj, the Allahabad Congress was attended by 1200 delegates including 200 Muslims.

The number of the delegates to the Congress rose further and almost reached the 1900 mark when the Congress held its next session in Bombay in December 1889 under the presidency of William Wedderburn, another British Liberal associated with the Congress Movement who later wrote the biography of Hume. It was at this session that Charles Bradlaugh who had already become the spokesman of India in the British Parliament was present and in consultation with the Congress leaders drafted a Bill for the expansion of the Legislative Councils in India, which he moved in the House of Commons in 1890. The British Government introduced a Bill of their own to counteract Bradlaugh's Bill and ultimately passed it in 1892 as the Indian Councils Act. The Act raised the number of additional members to a maximum of 16 for the Supreme Council, 20 for the Legislative Council of Bombay, Madras and Bengal and 15 for the North Western Provinces and Oudh, where a Legislative Council had been established in 1886. The Act which conceded to the members of the Legislative Councils the right of discussing the budget and asking questions on matters of public interest authorised the Governor-General-in Council to prescribe the method of appointing the additional members.

The Act of 1892 failed to satisfy the Congress leaders as the demand for the principle of direct election was not conceded and the number of additional members increased was very meagre. Yet it confirmed their faith in constitutional agitation to redress their grievances as it represented, despite humble and indirect, an outcome of such agitation since 1885. During all these past years the Congress leaders had been highlighting the political and economic grievances of the people of British India. The resolutions moved and passed at the Congress platform annually became later the subjects of animated discussion in the provincial conferences. The Indian press gave adequate coverage to the Congress proceedings. The Indian people became conscious of their own rights and privileges and realised the British Raj was not that "benevolent" as it claimed to be. The Congress leaders thus shook the very moral foundation of the British rule in India and now with the passing of the Indian Councils Act of 1892, their voices would be heard within the four walls of the Council Chambers also.

Chapter 11

Rise of the Extremists

In the decade that followed the passing of the Indian Councils Act of 1892, strains within the Indian National Congress began to develop. In 1892 Hume left for England with a prophecy of imminent peasant revolution unless the Congress leaders became more energetic and the British Raj more responsive. Hume who had been a General Secretary of the Congress continued to hold the post in the absence of a suitable substitute and the affairs of the Congress came largely to be dominated by the three legal trio—Surendra Nath Banerjea, W.C. Bonnerjee and Pherozeshah Mehta—till another legal luminary in the person of Gopal Krishna Gokhale rose as a new leader. These men were highly successful professionals who were unable to devote full time to the work of the Congress. For most of the Congress leaders, politics was a part-time affair. The local political associations which were largely dominated by lawyers met occasionally to elect from among themselves the Congress delegates for the year to pass resolutions on some immediate grievances. The Congress remained very much an elite organisation without mass support but with profound faith in constitutional agitation through prayers and petitions.

In the 1890s this moderate approach of prayers and petitions was challenged by a group of young leaders who derived their inspiration from Hindu religion, culture and history. They advocated bridging the gulf between the Congress and the masses through self-help, use of the vernaculars, utilization of traditional, popular customs and dress and institutions like the village fair or *mela*. Their reaction against the activities of the moderate leaders took three main forms: first, self-development through constructive work; second, passive resistance or mass mobilization for freedom through certain new techniques like boycott and third, revolutionary terrorism, which sought a short-cut to freedom through individual violence and conspiracies.

It was Aurobindo Ghosh, then living in Baroda, who first systematically criticised the moderate leadership of the Congress in 1893-94 in a series of articles entitled, "New Lamps for Old" in the *Induprakash.* Son of a Zamindar father, Ghosh was sent to England as a child for an Anglicised upbringing but he returned to India a dejected youngman after having failed at the riding test for the Civil Service examination. It was mainly because of his anti-British utterances for the British Raj's exploitation of India, news of which used to be sent to him by his father regularly, that this disqualification was imposed on Aurobindo. Once in Baroda, he began to react against his past life in England, which was to ultimately transform him into a saint much later. In the articles in the *Induprakash,* Aurobindo rejected the British model of slow constitutional progress admired by the Congress leaders in preference to the French model of the attainment of republic through violent means. He fiercely attacked the Congress mendicancy—prayers and petitions—and urged the widening of the Congress base by establishing close link between the Congress leadership and the proletariate. Aurobindo was no doubt influenced by the Hindu revivalism in Bengal since the mid- nineteenth century when Rajnarayan Basu's Hindu Nationalism led the "National Nabagopal Mitra" to organise Hindu *Mela* and the writings of Bankim Chandra Chatterji whose "Bandemataram" in *Anandamath* lent the title to his press organ later in Bengal. By the end of the nineteenth century, Aurobindo was trying to organise secret societies and actually sent Jatindranath Banerji and his younger brother, Barindra Kumar Ghosh to Bengal for the purpose.

However, Aurobindo's was not the only voice of disillusionment from Baroda with the Congress. In Bengal disillusionment with the Congress was expressed by Aswinikumar Dutta, Barisal school teacher with mass contact in his district through social work, who described the Amraoti session of the Congress in 1897 he attended, a "three days' *tamasha*". Rabindranath Tagore, already a leading literary figure in Bengal, voiced his disillusionment, through *swadeshi* enterprise and national education and made extremely perceptive suggestions for mass contact through *melas, jatras* and the use of vernaculars in both education and social work. And Vivekananda's message to the poor Indian masses to shed their cowardice and timidity and to feel bold, brave and free in an alien rule was given a more direct political colour by his disciple, the Irish Sister, Margaret Noble, Nivedita as Vivekananda called her, with her experience of Irish and other European revolutionary movements. The Western educated Bangalees were also turning to *swadeshi* industrial enterprise as could be seen from the foundation of Bengal Chemicals in 1893 in Calcutta by the scientist Acharya Profulla Chandra Roy. The *Dawn* editor, Satish Mukherjee through his Dawn Society and Tagore through his Bolepur Ashram had started experimentation with new forms of education under indigenous control. Thus extremism in Bengal was fanned more by the emergence of new historical forces than by the petty factionalism existing among the different political associations in Bengal.

In the Punjab, both Harkishan Lal who started the Punjab National Bank and the Arya Samajists of the College faction were very active in *swadeshi* enterprise from 1890 onwards. The Congress delegates from the Punjab expressed their dissatisfaction at the dominance of the Congress proceedings by the informal Bombay-Bengal axis and tried to break it by pressing for the formal constitution for the organisation from 1893 onwards. In his articles published in the *Kayastha Samachar*, Lajpat Rai argued for the introduction of the technical self-help in place of the annual festival of the English educated elite which was all that the Congress amounted to in his eyes. He also asked the Congrěss to base its organisation on the Hindus alone, as unity with the Mulsims was a day-dream of the Congress leaders.

However, the man who really blazed the trail of extremism in India was Bal Gangadhar Tilak who belonged to the Chitpavan Brahmins of Poona—a Maratha Brahmin of the class to which belonged the Peshwas. Born in 1866, Tilak graduated from the Bombay University and devoted his entire life to the service of his motherland. With W.G. Agarkar, Tilak founded two newspapers, one in English called the *Mahratta,* and the other in Marathi, called the *Kesari* which he himself edited from 1889 onwards. Tilak used religious orthodoxy as a method of mass contact through his alignment against reformers on the Age of Consent Bill in 1891, followed by the organisation of the Ganapati festival from 1894 and the development of patriotic-cum historical cult as a central symbol of nationalism through the Shivaji festival from 1896 onwords. He was the first to advise the peasants in Poona to withhold payment of land revenues when their crops failed in 1896-97 and called for *swadeshi* and boycott of British goods when Elgin imposed an excise duty on Indian cotton textiles. In his weeklies, the *Mahratta* and *Kesari* Tilak preached that the policy of the mendicancy of the Congress leaders must give way to that of assertion of Indian rights. "Freedom is my birth right", he observed. Referring to the annual session of the Congress, he wrote: "We will not achieve any success in our labours if we croak once a year like a frog." The peasants in the villages must be politically educated and brought within the fold of the Congress. "Then only will the Government realize," Tilak wrote, "that to despise the Congress is to despise the Indian nation. Then only will the efforts of the Congress leaders be crowned with success."

It was in the year 1897 that the difference in the two strategies of the Moderates and the Extremists illustrated itself. Within ten days of the Shivaji festival held at Poona on 12 June 1897, where Tilak had made fiery speeches, Rand, the Poona Collector and

Ayerst, another officer, were shot dead while returning from the Government House at night by the educated but unemployed Chapekar brothers, Damodar and Balkrishna, in order to avenge the atrocities committed by the British soldiers while enforcing the preventive measures against the epidemic of plague that had then broken out in Poona. Tilak was held responsible for indirectly inciting the Chapekar brothers to the murder by his defence of the murder of Afzal Khan by Shivaji in a *Kesari* article and was sentenced to 18 months' imprisonment. The proud disdain with which Tilak refused to offer an apology to the Raj for his fearless criticism of the repressive anti-plague measures was in marked contrast to the abject surrender of Gokhale who had tendered an apology to the Raj for statements made while in England against the violent acts of the British soldiers during the plague epidemic in Poona. Despite public sympathy expressed all over India for Tilak's arrest, the 1897 Amraoti session of the Congress dominated by the Moderates like Gokhale could not pass a special resolution about him though the Congress President, Sankaran Nair and the Indian Demosthenes, Surendra Nath Banerjea, paid eloquent tributes to him, not so much for Tilak's freedom but for freedom of the press which was at stake. Yet the trial and conviction of Tilak convinced the Indian people that what was needed now not eloquence but sacrifice, not orators but martyrs, for the cause of their motherland.

Chapter 12

Reaction of the Raj

With the murder of the two plague officers of Poona within ten days of Tilak's Shivaji festival on 12 June 1897, the British Raj swiftly swung into reaction. The murder convinced the Raj of the growth of an extremist faction within the Indian National Congress. "The more I see and hear of the National Congress Party," wrote Hamilton, the Secretary of State, to Elgin, the Viceroy, on 24 June 1897, "the more I am impressed with the seditious and double-sided character of the prime-movers of the organization." In 1898 the Raj passed the Sedition Law where sedition was clearly identified with the spread of education. For, after going through the papers leading to the Poona murders, Hamilton found it impossible to dissociate the Chapekar brothers' idea and hatred of England from the course of education and training through which they had passed and regarded the Ferguson College at Poona where Damodar and Balkrishna had studied as the mainspring of a small but deep-rooted political conspiracy in the Deccan.

In May 1899 Hamilton advised Curzon who had succeeded Elgin as the Viceroy in January 1899 to slow down the "Educational Juggernaut" by bringing higher education under effective control of the Raj. In September 1899, he further explained to Curzon that "the real danger to our rule in India" was "the gradual adoption and extension of Western agitation and organisation by the educated Indians." And with an obvious reference to the Congress which had developed two different outlooks in the past one decade, he observed: "If we could break the Hindu educated party into two sections holding widely different views, we should, by such a division, strengthen our position against the subtle and continuous attack which the spread of education make upon our present system of Government."

Curzon's intelligence reported to him of the sad state of decline in which the Congress had fallen. The Congress now-a-days was dominated by the local delegates and there was a perceptible decline in the activities of the Poona Sarvajanik Sabha, the Indian Association of Calcutta and the Mahajana Sabha of Madras. He was also convinced that the spread of English education in India since the days of Macaulay was "a story of grave political miscalculation" and had given birth to a tone of mind and to a type of character that was "ill-regulated, averse from discipline, discontented, and in some cases actually disloyal." If the number of such discontented young educated persons could be checked by a check on the spread of higher education in India, the Congress would die a natural death. "My own belief is," Curzon informed Hamilton in November 1900, "that the Congress is tottering to its fall, and one of my greatest ambitions while in India is to assist it to a peaceful demise."

By November 1900 when Curzon wrote to Hamilton about one of his greatest ambitions while in India, he had made substantial progress in his plan for bringing higher education under government control. What sort of reform he had been contemplating could be seen from one of his earlier actions regarding Ripon's local self-government in India. In July 1899 he had passed the Calcutta Municipality Act which reduced the size of the Calcutta Corporation from 75 to 50 Commissioners by taking away 25 seats of elected members. The former two-thirds majority of elected members was thus eliminated and nominated members, forming a pro-government party, became the controlling factor in the Corporation with the support of the official Chairman. Such a step was absolutely uncalled for from the Indian point of view, for the Calcutta Corporation though dominated by the popular representatives had been doing "excellent work" and in protest the 28 elected members including Surendra Nath Banerjea resigned from the Corporation saying that the Calcutta Municipality Act had made a "Mockery of Local Self-Government."

In September 1901 Curzon summoned a Conference at Simla of "some 15-16 educational experts" including Directors of Public Instruction and Vice-Chancellors of the five universities from all parts of India to discuss the question of university reform. On 2 September Curzon displayed great skill in his inaugural address to the Conference where he "absolutely ignored the political dangers of the present system, and based the necessity for reform upon educational grounds alone." On 10 September the deliberations were over, the delegates having passed unanimously on the subject of university education no fewer than 45 resolutions, each one of which was drafted by Curzon himself. The delegates emphatically declared in favour of a thorough constitutional reform of the universities in India. They also recommended that the powers of government in respect of affiliation, recognition and textbooks should be strengthened; that a Director-General of Indian education should be appointed; that the rules for examinations and degrees should be co-ordinated and improved, and that the institution of hostels should be encouraged and that a minimum rate of fees should be fixed. The Conference was also in favour of the decision to which Curzon had already come before the deliberations at Simla started that it was desirable to appoint a Commission to examine the question of university education in all its aspects. No Indian educational expert, despite the suggestion of one official Indian name to Curzon by MacDonnel, the Lt. Governor of the North-Western Provinces, was invited to the Conference. The opening speech was released to the press but the proceedings were never published. The secrecy with which Curzon enveloped the Conference at Simla earned for it such designations as Secret

Conclave and Star Chamber. As Surendra Nath Banerjea later remarked sarcastically: "The Conference met in secret, deliberated in secret, resolved in secret, and I presume dispersed in secret." The Indian press and the people, the session of the Congress in Calcutta in December 1901, clamoured for the representation of the Indian interests on the forthcoming Indian Universities Commission.

When the Indian Universities Commission was set up next year with Raleigh, the Vice-Chancellor of the Calcutta University as the Chairman, its membership did include only one Indian out of five Europeans and the Indian included was Syed H. Bilgrami whose "hostile attitude towards the educated classes of India" was too well-known through his writings and speeches. Banerjea through the columns of the *Bengalee* raised "a vigorous protest" against the absence of a Hindu member among the six permanent Commissioners since the Hindus had "the largest interest in the educational problems that were to be considered." The great stir created among the Hindus had its effect and Gooroodas Banerjee, a judge of the Calcutta High Court and a former Vice-Chancellor of the Calcutta University was added to the list of six.

The Indian Universities Commission which was assisted by five local Commissioners in the collection of their evidences in Bengal, Bombay, Madras, North-Western Provinces and the Punjab submitted its report within five months of its appointment and its recommendations faithfully reflected the decisions taken at the Simla Conference last year. The Commission suggested that "a General Indian University Act" be passed to give effect to the changes reflected by the recommendations. Gooroodas Banerje found himself unable to agree with the recommendations and submitted "a Note of Dissent."

When Curzon was awaiting the approval of the Home Government for making the recommendations public, a copy of the report of the Raleigh Commission was leaked to the press. A series of daily denunciations of the Raj followed and Curzon was credited with "having rung the death-knell of higher education in India." In the meeting at the Albert Hall, Calcutta, organised by Surendra Nath Banerjea who drafted a memorial for presentation to Curzon, "old men, bent down with the weight of years, the representatives of an older school of thought and culture, the products of our pre-university system, came tottering to place on record their protest against the recommendations of the Commission." All classes of people who had hitherto benefited from higher education in India joined this protest movement. Former servants of the British Raj who had once served the government, with great honour and credit and who were now leading their quiet lives away from the storm and stress of the political agitation, could not but emerge from their seclusion to join those who had already condemned the report. Professional men who had never before spoken at a public meeting and who had never identified themselves with any movement of any kind now forgot their professions and their profits and joined the people in their protest against the report. The Muslims who had been somewhat backward in public movements had been most forward in condemning the report. They had promptly disavowed the representative character of the only Muslim member of the Commission, Bilgrami, and denounced him for signing a report which they rightly believed would be fatal to the educational interests of their Community.

From Bengal the agitation moved to "other parts of India." In Trichinopoly, the undergraduate students of S.P.G. College unanimously passed resolutions emphatically protesting against the Commission's recommendations on the second grade colleges. Similarly in North Arcot the Muslim Community passed resolutions against the recommendations of the Commission. In Bombay the agitation against the report of the Commission was mainly organised by Pherozehsah Mehta. "The great importance of the subject," observed Mehta, "demanded a different treatment, and it can be no matter for complaint if the recommendations of the Commission have no more weight attached to them than those of any other seven men throughout the kingdom of equivalent qualifications, of whom there are hundreds, on subjects on which the most eminent men of English and Continental universities are not yet agreed." Observing about the turmoil that followed the publication of the recommendations of the Indian Universities Commission, Banerjea said in his presidential address at the Ahmedabad Congress on 23 December 1902: "I do not remember any proposal, emanating from responsible authority, which has more profoundly stirred the hearts of the Indian community, or has caused deeper alarm, or evoked more strenuous opposition than the Report of the Universities Commission. The opposition to the Vernacular Press Act, to the Calcutta Municipal Bill, the Bombay Land Revenue Bill or even the Sedition Bill pales before the agitation which the Report of the Universities Commission gave rise to. There was a sense of alarm, deep, genuine, all-pervading felt by all sections of the educated community throughout India, by Hindoos and Mussulmans alike."

The "fierce agitation" as described by Curzon to Hamilton in September 1902 led the former to seek the opinion of the local governments on some of the recommendations of the Commission, which had exicted the strongest opposition from the Indian community. The Ahmedabad Congress thanked Curzon for the issue of the circular letter to the local governments but pointed out that the Congress viewed "with the gravest alarm" many of the Commission's recommendations, the acceptance of which would, in its opinion, "reverse the policy steadily pursued during the last half a century by the British Government in the matter of higher education, by checking its spread and restricting its scope, and by virtually destroying such limited independence as the universities at present" enjoyed.

When the Congress was hammering at the recommendations of the Indian Universities Commission, Curzon was busy with the Draft Bill. The Draft Bill emerged after Curzon had minuted on the notes on university education prepared by Denzil Ibbetson, Risley and Orange, the newly appointed Director-General of Education, and was introduced into the Legislative Council at Simla in November 1903. Before the Legislative Council at Calcutta resumed the discussion on the Bill ignoring the fervent appeal of the Madras Congress in December 1903 for its "abandonment," on 10 March 1904, Curzon had passed the official Secrets Act on 4 March— a sequel to the leakage of the recommendation of the Indian Universities Commission to the press and to make the case for reform of higher education look stronger issued the State Paper on Indian Education on 11 March to show the proposed university reform as a part of the Raj's general scheme of reforms on education, mentioning the financial aid, without which "the necessary improvement in the universities and their affiliated colleges" could not be carried out. Despite the opposition provided at every stage of the passage of the Bill by Gokhale and Asutosh Mukhopadhyaya, the Bill was passed with the help of the European and the nominated Indian members, Bepin Krishna Bose and R.G.Bhandarkar. And Curzon wrote to Godley, the Under-Secretary of State, in a relaxed mood on 24 March 1904: "Here I have had the stiffest session on record, and have carried the Universities Bill, which was my child."

However, despite Curzon's success in passing the Indian Universities Act of 1904 strictly according to his plan as we have seen, his university reform boomeranged on him. They excited the very flames of Indian nationalism, which he was out to extinguish. "The storms in a tea cup" about which Curzon wrote to Godley after the Legislative Council had passed the Indian Universities Validating Act in February 1905, turned out to be storms in an ocean, raising turbulent waves of Indian nationalism, when Curzon adamantly went ahead with "the contemplated partition of Bengal."

Chapter 13

Partition of Bengal

Since the grant by Shah Alam in 1765 of the Diwani of Bengal, Bihar and Orissa to the East India Company, each successive addition of company's territory in the north was added to it so that by 1810 it was already unwieldy stretching up to Delhi and beyond to the Sikh frontier. The Charter Act of 1833 provided for the creation of another presidency—the North-Western Provinces out of the unwieldy Bengal Presidency with its capital at Agra under a Lt. Governor and in 1854 Bengal, Bihar and Orissa— the Bengal proper— was placed under a Lt. Governor in immediate subordination to the Governor-General. In 1874 Assam with three Bengali speaking districts of Sylhet, Cachar and Goalpara was withdrawn from the Lieutenant Governorship of Bengal and placed under a Chief Commissioner. In 1896 the Assam Chief Commissioner, William Ward, prepared a scheme of partition whereby Chittagong division and Dacca and Mymensing districts of Bengal would be added to Assam to form a Lt. Governor's province to further the interests of the civil servants. The idea was dropped because of the protest of Chittagong backed by the rest of Bengal but was revived in 1900 when the Assam tea-planters emphasised to Curzon the need of a port nearer than Calcutta to escape the prohibitive freight charges made by the Assam Bengal Railway and two years later in 1902 when Curzon was called upon to solve the problem of Berar, a newly acquired territory on perpetual lease from the Nizam of Hyderabad: "Ought Chittagong to continue to belong to it [Bengal], or ought we to give Assam an outlet on the sea?" Curzon asked this question in a broader perspective. By that time the population of Bengal had reached 78 million and the Bengal Lt. Governor, Andrew Fraser, proposed to reduce it by giving Orissa to the Central Provinces. At this Curzon asked Fraser to prepare a comprehensive plan of redistribution of boundaries of Bengal and her neighbouring countries.

Fraser who had been a witness to Bengal politics for many years past felt that certain districts of Bengal had become "a hot-bed of the purely Bengali movement unfriendly if not seditious in character." Both the Calcutta leaders and the Calcutta newspapers had established a tyranny in these areas, which should be immediately scotched. He revived Ward's scheme of 1896 with slight additions without informing Curzon of the trouble it had run into. Risley, the Home Secretary to the Government of India, supported Fraser'scheme, as he felt the preponderance of the Bengalis in provincial politics was "most desirable" to diminish and this could best be achieved by dividing them as proposed by Fraser: "Bengal united is a power. Bengal divided will pull several different ways. That is what the Congress leaders feel: their apprehensions are perfectly correct and they form one of the great merits of the scheme." In this context Risley referred to the case of the Marathi speaking Berar which was joined with the Central Provinces, instead of the Bombay Presidency where Curzon heard "quite enough of Shivaji as it is" and commented: "It is not altogether easy to reply in a dispatch which is sure to be published without disclosing the fact that in this scheme as in the matter of the amalgamation of Berar to the Central Provinces one of our main objects is to split up and thereby to weaken a solid body of opponents to our rule." Thus the scheme which began as an administrative necessity later developed into a political tool in the hands of the British Raj to destroy a people not only ethnically but also culturally. Curzon emphasised how the eastern districts of the

Chapter 14

Swadeshi and Swaraj

When the partition of Bengal was effected on 16 October 1905, it was observed as a day of national mourning for the whole of Bengal. There was hardly a home in Bengal which was not aware of the event because of imaginative appeals made by Rabindranath Tagore for *Rakhi Bandhan* and by Ramendrasunder Trivedi for *Arandhan.* Bengalees tied *Rakhi* to one another's wrists as symbol of brotherhood and fasted as sign of mourning. There was a general hartal. Shops and markets remained closed, vehicular traffic ceased and life came to a standstill. In the evening a mammoth public meeting presided over by A.M Bose at the Calcutta Town Hall laid the foundation of the Federation Hall which was to be "the mark and symbol of their indivisible union." After the meeting was over, a large procession was taken out to the north of the city and there another meeting was held where a large sum of money was raised for the successful operation of the Anti-Partition Movement.

The partition of Bengal was an insult to the sense of unity and of pride developed among the Bengalees ever since the beginning of the nineteenth century Bengal Renaissance. The capital of Bengal which was also the capital of British India had benefited the Bengalees most. Taking advantage of the new education the Bengalees had established a lead in professions, government services and politics over much of India. An Indian poet, Rabindranath Tagore who was on the threshold of world new province would be freed from "the pernicious influence of Calcutta" and their Muslim population would get a better and juster deal in a minute on the Fraser's scheme on 1 June 1903 which after receiving the assent of the Secretary of State was published as Risley Paper on 3 December 1903.

Since the new province would be placed under a Chief Commissioner, many Bengalees would be deprived of the privileges and facilities of possessing a Legislative Council, a Board of Revenue and a High Court at Calcutta. The Congress in its December 1903 session denounced the scheme as "preposterous" for besides involving the administration in huge expenses, it would undo the unity of India and endanger the communal amity between the Hindus and the Muslims. At this Curzon wrote to Brodrick: "If we are weak enough to yield to their clamour now, we shall not be able to dismember or reduce Bengal again; and you will be cementing and solidifying, on the eastern flank of India, a force already formidable and certain to be a source of increasing trouble in the future." Curzon developed the Risley Plan further in Mymensing in February 1904 when he proposed to include in the new province the whole of Rajsahi division except Darjeeling, Dacca division and Chittagong division. He told the Muslim audience at Dacca that one of the reasons for partition was "to invest the Mohammedans in Eastern Bengal with a unity which they have not enjoyed since the days of the old Mussulman Viceroys and Kings." Advised by Risley to build the new province on the foundation of communalism, Curzon roped in Nawab Salimullah Khan of Dacca by promising him a loan of £ 100,000 at nominal interest and the Nawab had little difficulty in organising huge Muslim gathering to support Curzon's plan for a new province for the Muslims in Bengal.

The communal implications of the plan were thoroughly exposed at the Calcutta Town Hall meetings of 18 March 1904 and the Congress President Cotton was refused an interview by Curzon who had just returned to India after a brief sojourn in England for his second term as the Viceroy. For nearly one year since Curzon's development of the Risley Plan in Mymensing in February 1904, there was a complete lull and the Congress which was then reeling under the blows delivered by Curzon's Indian Universities Act of March 1904 was led to believe that "the project of partition" had been abandoned. On 2 February 1905 Curzon sent home his partition plan. The Secretary of State's India Council which was aware of the bitterness created by it asked Curzon to consider a separate plan to relieve the Lt. Governor of Bengal by putting a few districts of Bengal, say Chotanagpur and Orissa under a Commissioner "with powers of a Lt. Governor." This was vehemently opposed by Curzon: "The best guarantee of the political advantage of our proposal is its dislike by the Congress Party." The Council accepted most reluctantly Curzon's plan and Brodrick expressed his own qualms of conscience on 9 June 1905: "That a large and upon the whole homogeneous community of 41½ millions, with Calcutta as their centre of culture and political and commercial life, should object to the transfer of 3/5 of their number to a new administration with a distant capital, involving the severance of old and historic ties and the breaking up of racial unity, appears to me in no way surprising."

The resolution on partition drafted by Curzon himself was published on 19 July 1905 and on 10 October while publishing the partition papers after judicious pruning, the British Government requested Curzon to postpone its promulgation for another three weeks, but Curzon was not prepared to brook any further delay. The partition of Bengal was made effective on 16 October.

recognition was a Bengalee and another Indian, Vivekananda who had carried the message of Hinduism triumphantly to the West was also a Bengalee. A self-confidence among the Bengalees was thus growing which was often wounded by the racial discrimination of the British Raj and they often found solace in such international events as the British reverses in the Boer War, the spectacular Japanese victory over Russia in 1904-5 which proved that a "dwarf" Asian country like Japan could also beat a "giant" European one like Russia.

The partition affected all classes of Bengalees. Already as estimated by Valentine Chirol, there were some 40,000 educated unemployed youngmen in the Bengal before partition. The educated Bengalees in the new province were now worried about their chances of landing clerical jobs in Calcutta. Zamindars with estates in both Bengals were now faced with the unavoidable problem of appointing two sets of agents and pleaders, the Calcutta lawyers were afraid that a new province would ultimately mean another High Court which would cut into their practice and the Bengalee merchants with raw-jute and trading interests in Calcutta were jealous of the possible rise of Chittagong as a commercial centre. And finally the Bengalee politicians found their chances of winning a seat in the Legislative Councils of both the provinces dim as they found themselves in a minority being outnumbered in one by the Biharis and the Oriyas and in the other by the Muslims and the Assamese.

The anguish and anger of the people of Bengal was given expression by Rabindranath Tagore, Rajani Kanta Sen, Dwijendralal Roy and Mukunda Das. Besides tuning Bankim's *Bande Mataram* which was on every body's lips, Tagore composed innumerable songs, breathing through every note a warm, nostalgic and poignant love which dedicated life and soul to the cause of the motherland. Ramsay MacDonald, then a visitor to Bengal, wrote in the *Daily Chronicle* of London, how Bengal was creating India "by song and worship" and Ezra Pound observed how "Tagore has sung Bengal into a nation." The people of Bengal rose like one man to resist, to suffer and to sacrifice and besides Calcutta, the mofussil districts like Barisal and Mymensingh were soon caught in the fire of patriotism. A new tone, a new perspective, a new dimension was added to the national movement hitherto unknown in India and for all this, as Gokhale acknowledged in his presidential address at the Benares Congress which condemned the partition of Bengal emphatically, "India owes a deep debt of gratitude to Bengal." Spearheaded by the students who represented youth and dream, vigour and selfless dedication and joined by the workers and the peasants, the clerks and the teachers who had been affected most by the rising prices since 1904, the Anti-Partition Movement soon broke away from traditional moorings and after transcending its rather limited and immediate objective broadened into a struggle for *Swaraj* developing a variety of important techniques in the process.

Two such important techniques were those of boycott and *Swadeshi* which got a new impetus from the Anti-Partition Movement. However, the concepts were not new. As early as 1870 Bholanath Chandra had recommended boycott of British goods to bring pressure on the British Raj and Tilak, as we already have seen, led a full-fledged boycott campaign in 1896-97. Similarly, *Swadeshi* as a purely economic measure for the development of Indian Industry, had been preached by Gopalrao Deshmukh of Poona in 1849, Rajnarayan Bose and Nabagopal Mitra in the 1860s, G.V. Joshi and M.V. Ranade of Bombay and Rabindranath Tagore in the 1890s.

However, the Moderates and the Extremists differed from each other in their interpretation of the concepts of boycott and *Swadeshi*. The Bombay Moderates like Gokhale considered boycott as a political weapon used for a definite political purpose. The Bengal Moderates like Banerjea considered boycott to be a last desperate attempt to get partition revoked by pulling at the purse-strings of Manchester. They were afraid of alienating the well-wishers among the Englishmen. Not so were the Extremists. With Aurobindo, Bipin Chandra Pal and Tilak, boycott became the starting point for the formulation of a whole range of new dogmas and methods leading to *Swaraj*. Boycott would not merely be confined to non- consumption of British goods but would embrace in its purview the whole field of government. It would make administration under present conditions impossible by an organised refusal to do anything which would help either British commerce in the exploitation of the country or British officialdom in the administration of it. For Aurobindo, the end of boycott as the revocation of the partition only was "the pettiest and narrowest of all political objects." A religious colour was added to the concept of boycott when Banerjea initiated *Swadeshi* vow in temples, Tilak described boycott as "political Yoga" and the *Sandhya* talked of Liverpool salt and Mauritus sugar as being refined with bone dust of swine and kine.

The Benares Congress under the presidency of Gokhale endorsed *Swadeshi* and boycott for Bengal but did not approve of a boycott for the whole of India. Lajpat Rai asked other provinces to follow the example of Bengal, and Tilak pointed out that the basic goal of boycott and *Swadeshi* was the attainment of Swaraj. The call for boycott and S*wadeshi* was given at thousands of public meetings—in Bengal the first call was however given by the *Sanjivani* on 22 June after the plan for partition had received the assent of Brodrick on 9 June, followed by the Town Hall meeting under the presidency of N.N. Sen on 7 August and Banerjea's *Bengalee* on 12 August. Public meetings and processions, picketing, patriotic songs, bonfire of foreign goods and fiery speeches kept the spirit of nationalism through boycott and *Swadeshi* burning at white heat. The boycott and *Swadeshi* programmes were interlinked. As has been aptly said, "the Boycott was the negative, the *Swadeshi* the positive, aspect of the same idea." While British goods were boycotted, were burnt, at public places and shops selling them were picketed, a vigorous drive was made for the production and sale of *Swadeshi* goods, largely through the effort of students.

In Bengal the British crackdown on students picketers through Carlye Circular on 22 October 1905 which threatened to withdraw grants, scholarship and affiliation from the nationalist dominated institutions climaxed the urge for the boycott of government controlled education—an urge which had been growing in Bengal ever since the appointment of the Indian Universities Commission in 1902, the creation of the Dawn Society by Satish Chandra Mukherjee, and the passing of the Indian Universities Act in 1904. Within a month of the Carlyle circular, the Anti-Circular Society was born on 4 November 1905, presided over by Krishnakumar Mitra of the *Sanjivani* and critically sympathised by Tagore. The Moderates like Banerjea, Bhupendranath Basu and Astutosh Chaudhuri combined with the Extremists like Bipin Chandra Pal, Motilal Chosh and Brahmabandhav who described the government controlled Calcutta University as the house of slaves at Goldighi, in organising a National Council of Education financed by the Zamindars of Mymensingh and leading lawyers like Subodh Chandra Mallick which was formally inaugurated on 14 August 1906 with the foundation of the Bengal National College.

The College which was founded with Aurobindo as the Principal, was largely due to the labours of Satish Chandra Mukherjee of the Dawn Society set up in July 1902 and his young followers who formed the nucleus of its teaching staff. Vernacular was to be the chief medium of instruction but foreign languages were not to be neglected. Scientific and technical education were calculated to develop the material resources of the country and to satisfy its pressing needs. Unfortunately the National Council of Education could not retain its unity for long and the Moderates headed by Taraknath Palit set tip a rival organisation called the Society for the Promotion of Technical Education which founded a college, the Bengal Technical Institute.

This *Swadeshi* mood led to the launching of the Banga Lakshmi Cotton Mills in August 1906 with equipment brought from an existing Serampore plant and led to the revival of cottage industries like handloom, silk-weaving and some other traditional artisan crafts. There were some fairly successful ventures in porcelain like the Calcutta Pottery Works set up in 1906, chrome tanning, soap, matches and cigarettes. These were financed not only by big zamindars like Manindra Nandi of Kasimbazar but also by professional intellectuals like Nilratan Sarkar and Profulla Chandra Roy who had earlier set up his Bengal Chemicals in Calcutta. The same spirit of *Swadeshi* led J.N. Tata who founded the Tata Iron and Steel in 1907 with the entire capital of £ 16,30,000 fully subscribed by 8,000 Indians within three months. In the United Provinces the British Raj appeared sympathetic towards the *Swadeshi* of Malaviya and Chintamani who had not responded to Tilak's U.P. tour in January 1907. Both were invited to the officially sponsored Industrial Conference at Naini Tal in 1907 for the protection of the U.P. sugar. In the Punjab the *Swadeshi* atmosphere revived the interests of its well-established traditional business communities in the fields of indigenous banking, insurance and education and in Tuticorin in October 1906 a *Swadeshi* Steam Navigation Company which was started with a capital of rupees six lakh to run steamers up to Colombo aroused bitter hostility of the British India Steam Navigation Company. In Andhra Delta towns like Rajamundhry, Kakinada and Masulipatam police repression on students which followed wearing the *Bande Mataram* badges and attending of Bipin Chandra Pal's meetings in April 1907 led to a boycott of government controlled schools and colleges. The *Swadeshi* spirit started a movement for national schools in Andhra and created a new interest in Telugu language, literature and history. Similarly in Poona the *Swadeshi* atmosphere led to revival of the Ganapati and Shivaji festivals started by Tilak in 1890s, boycott and bonfires of foreign cloth and as in October 1905 at Poona, it led to a great enthusiasm for indigenous cloth which fetched huge profits for the Textile Mill owners of Bombay and Ahmedabad and a *Swadeshi Vastu Pracharini Sabha* was set up in the Bombay city itself, still a citadel of the Moderate leaders like Mehta and Gokhale.

The message of boycott and *Swadeshi* began to reach the masses, and they would have responded more vigorously had the Extremists called upon the peasants to start a no-rent campaign or the workers to strike against the capitalists. There were disturbances involving the indigo ryots of Champaran in Bihar and the peasants of Assam and of the new province of Bengal. Aswini Kumar Dutta led the Muslim peasants of Barisal in their agitations and Lajpat Rai was deported in May 1907 for inspiring the Chenab colonists of Muslims, Sikhs and Hindus in their no-rent campaign against the Punjab Government. The boycott concept spread infection more in the ranks of factory clerks, workers and artisans. A wave of strikes broke out in Bengal in late 1905 and early 1906 engulfing the Burn Iron works, Government Presses, Settlement Department in Barisal, the Railway Workshop at Jamalpur, Clive Jute Mills and Fort Gloucester Jute Mills. The *Bande Mataram* supported the cause of Jute Mills labourers. A year later bigger strikes swept the East Bengal Railway and the Oudh and Rohilkund Railway and in April 1908 the employees of the Calcutta Telegraph went on strike. The Pheonix Mill in Bombay went on strike in October 1905, followed by the Railway Workshop at Parel in May 1907. In Bombay where the major part of the factory workers came from Tilak's own home district of Ratnagiri, mass picketing of liquor shops and boycott of foreign cloths organised by Tilak were highly successful. When Tilak was convicted on 22 July 1908 for certain *Kesari* articles on Bengal terrorism, and given six years' transportation, the cloth shop employees of the Mulji Jetha Market gave a call for a hartal of six days—one for each year of Tilak's imprisonment—a vow which the workers of 76 out of 85 Textile Mills of Bombay as well as the Railway Workshop of Parel kept till 28 July by staging a massive walk out. In Tuticorin, the workers of the Coral Cotton Mills, inspired by Subramania Siva and Chidambaran Pillai who preached *Swaraj,* boycott and Russian

Revolution, went on strike and obtained a rise in wages by the first week of March 1908. British efforts in mid-March to prosecute Siva and Pillai led to protest strikes by the shop keepers, municipal and private sweepers and carriage drivers in Tuticorin and attacks on municipal offices, law courts and police stations in Tirunelveli. There were firing in both towns by the police. The *Bande Mataram* on 13 March 1908 hailed these events as forging a "bond between the educated class and masses, which is the first great step towards Swaraj."

The ideas of *Swadeshi* and boycott were preached by the radical press, like the *Sandhya* edited by Brahmabandhab Upadhaya, the *Yugantar* edited by Bhupendranath Dutta, the *Bande Mataram* edited by Aurobindo Ghosh, the *Kesari* edited by Tilak and the *Punjabi* edited by Lajpat Rai as well as by the various *Sabhas* and *Samitis* which down to the summer of 1908 were open bodies engaged in various activities including the method of implementing the techniques of boycott or passive resistance. As the police repression of Bampfyld Fuller in Eastern Bengal and Assam virtually let loose a reign of terror described by the *Manchester Guardian* as "Petty--fogging tyranny" which Russia could not "afford", they went underground and took to terrorist activities. Besides the criminal Law Amendment Act of December 1908 which banned the principal *Samitis* in Bengal, other aspects of the British Raj's regressive policy were the Seditious Meetings Act of 1907 which severely restricted the right of holding public meetings, the Explosive Substances Act of 1908 which prescribed heavy penalty for possessing materials for manufacturing bombs, the Newspapers Act of 1908 which placed the existence of a newspaper at the mercy of the Magistrate. We have already noted, the deportation of Laipat Rai and Ajit Singh in May 1907, trial and transportation of Tilak for six years in July 1908 and now the Act banning the *Samits* in Bengal also deported in December nine Bengalee leaders including Aswini Kumar Dutta, Krishna Kumar Mitra, Pulinbehari Das and Suhodh Chandra Mullick.

Apart from 19 *Samitis* in Calcutta, there were five principal *Samitis* in the districts of Dacca, Mymemsingh, Faridpur, Bakargunj and Barisal–they were *Swadesh, Bandhav, Sadhana, Brati, Dacca Anushilan* and *Suhrid.* The Anti-Circular Society was the only Samiti in Calcutta which included many important Muslim associates. In the new province, it was the Barisal based *Swadesh Bandhav* of Aswini Kumar Dutta which acquired remarkable popularity among the peasants both Hindu and Muslim of the district, through the sustained humanitarian work of the leader as in the famine of 1906. It, however, disappeared as soon as the police repression began. The Dacca based *Anushilan Samiti* of Pulinbehari Das concentrated from the very beginning on secret training of cadres through physical culture and a paraphernalia of initiation vows steeped in Hinduism. However, it was the well-organised Dacca model which survived police repression and stepped in the footsteps of the Irish terrorists and the Russian Nihilists. It must however be mentioned here that inspired by the Poona incident of 1897 the first terrorist group was started in Midnapare in 1902 by Jnanendranath Bose.

In 1906 at the advice of Aurobindo, an inner circle within the Calcutta *Anushilan Samiti* under Barindra Kumar Ghosh and Bhupendranath Dutta brought out the *Yugantar* and when the Barisal Provincial Conference on April 1906 presided over by Abdul Rasul was broken up by a police lathi-charge, *Yugantar* wrote: "The remedy lies with the people themselves. The 30 crores of people inhabiting India must raise their 60 crores of hands to stop this curse of oppression. Force must be stopped by force." The Yugantar Party attempted some abortive actions like a plan to kill the very unpopular Lt. Governor of Eastern Bengal and Assam, Fuller, which misfired. In January 1908 Hemchandra Kanungo, after obtaining military training from a Russian emigre in Paris, set up on his return to India, a bomb factory camouflaged under a religious school at a garden house in Maniktala, Calcutta. It was detected within hours of the Kennedy murders on 30 April 1908 by Kshudiram Basu and Prafulla Chaki and the whole group including Aurobindo were arrested. Basu and Chaki missed their target — a notorious unpopular Calcutta magistrate named Kingsford. The conspiracy case against Aurobindo and his group was interrupted by the killing of the approver, the officers in charge of the investigation and of the prosecution. While Aurobindo was acquitted because of the brilliant pleading of his counsel, C.R. Das, four others including his brother Barindra Kumar were deported to the Andamans. Khudiram Basu, together with Kanailal Dutta and Satyen Basu who had killed the approver, were hanged. Aurobindo went to Pondicherry after the Alipur Bomb Case and the extremism in Bengal lost much of its punch when Aurobindo announced his decision to give up politics.

In Maharashtra after Tilak had been imprisoned, the Nasik based Abhinava Bharat which came into existence in 1907 out of *Mitra Me!a* founded in 1899, used the pistols sent secretly by V. D. Savarkar from London, to kill the Nasik District Magistrate Jackson, in December 1909. A similar society in Gwalior proclaimed its goal to be a republic against the autocracy of Sindhia who was a British puppet. In the United Provinces a revolutionary group formed at Benares consisted of student recruits like Sundar Lal who were quickly drawn into terrorism while in the Punjab after the removal of Lajpat Rai terrorism emerged. Ajit Singh, uncle of Bhagat Singh, organized *Anjuman-i-Mohibban-i-Watan* in Lahore with a few Arya Samajists like Bhai Paramanand and the brilliant Delhi student from St. Stephen's College, Har Dayal. In Madras after the removal of Siva and Pillai whose activities we have already noted, a revolutionary group emerged in Tirunelveli which was responsible for the murder of the District Magistrate, Ashe, in June 1911. The group included a major young poet whose fiery poems contributed much to the emergence of Tamil nationalism. He was Subramaniya Bharati who died in 1921 at a very young age of 39.

Thus the Anti-Partition Movement which started with the Moderates at the wheels went out of their control as soon as it gathered momentum. It developed from *Swadeshi to Swaraj.* And for the first time in the history of the anti-Raj agitations in India, it widened its base by inviting and attracting new participants, peasants and workers, though mass participation of these grass root people was yet to become a full scale reality. Workers in Calcutta and Bombay and peasants in Barisal and the Punjab indeed made some signicant contributions to the movement but the Extremists failed to rouse them inspite of all talk of "appeal to the masses" because they had nothing yet to offer to them. As before, the brunt of the movement fell on the students. "It was the fervour of the students", wrote Banerjea, "that communicated itself to the whole community and inspired it with an impulse the like of which had never been felt before." The students formed national volunteer groups and marched out of government schools and colleges, shouting *Bande Mataram,* singing national songs, picketing shops or selling *Swadashi* goods. Police repression followed by anger and desperation led many of them to join secret societies and take to terrorist activities. Their desperate deeds and daring plans, cool action and indifference to death won many of them a lasting place in the memory of the nation. And finally, the Extremist leaders failed to visualise India as a country with many people belonging to various castes, creeds and classes, as had been earlier realised by the Moderate leaders. Tilak and Aurobindo put too much faith on Hinduism and their appeal to Hindu religion often proved disastrous though men like Abdul Rasul and Liakat Hossain marched with the Hindu opponents of the partition and suffered equally. The Hindu tinge imparted to the movement weakened the process of national unification and was to contribute to the bitter harvest of communalism in later years.

Yet it cannot be denied that the real awakening of India, as Gandhi has observed, "took place after the partition of Bengal. After the partition, people saw that petitions must be backed up by force, and that they must be capable of suffering." The suffering of the people sustained the humble masses who could not imitate those immortals who embraced gallows as bridal garlands. The mighty upsurge did not die down with the repeal of the partition in 1911 by Hardinge. And when the Home Rule Movement began after a few years and when Gandhi appeared on the scene in 1919 and gave a call for a non-violent struggle, India was ready. She rose from her villages and cities, no longer afraid to die, for her men and women had learnt the mystery of life and death from the men and women of 1905-11.

Chapter 15

Muslim League

The Aligarh Muslim saw in the partition of Bengal an opportunity to fertilise the seeds of the two-nation theory of Syed Ahmad Khan who had founded in 1893 the Muhammedan Anglo-Oriental Defence Association of Upper India to safeguard the interests of the Muslims from the Congress Movement. A separate administration, a separate High Court and a separate university at Dacca would give extra opportunity to the Muslims to emerge from their backward state and weaken the economic base of the Hindu middle class. The Hindu zamindar patrons of the Congress would find the Muslim peasantry ranged against them, secure in support of the Dacca Secretariat.

However, the Anti-Partition Movement concealed the cleavage when Muslims with Catholic views like Abdul Rasul and Liakat Hossain joined the Congress leaders in their crusades against the partition and on 13 May 1906 the Muslim residents of Calcutta strongly condemned the repressive measures used to break up the April Barisal Conference under the presidency of Abdul Rasul. Inspired by the Muslim revolutionary activities of Egypt, Iran and Turkey, Abul Kalam Azad came into contact with Shyamsundar Chakravarti, met Aurobindo and joined one of the revolutionary bodies in Bengal. Azad not only dissipated the anti-Muslim suspicions of the revolutionaries but helped in extending their activities outside Bengal and Bihar. Azad also started his work among Muslims and found that a group of youngmen were "ready to take up the new political tasks."

Minto who had succeeded Curzon as the Viceroy was duly warned of the dangers of a Hindu Muslim accord by diehard bureaucrats like Lawrence, formerly Private Secretary to Curzon and shrewd journalists like Valentine Chirol and Sydney Low. And Theodore Morison, the Principal of the Aligarh College, warned the British Government in London against "the possibility of Mohammedan sympathies by going over to the Congress Party." In turn Minto was warned by Morley against such a possibility.

Minto's task was made easier by Fuller who as the Lt. Governor of the new province was pursuing a policy of divide and rule by calling the Muslim community his favourite wife, *Suo Rani.* Unwillingly also in their attempt to extend the Anti-Partition Movement to rural areas, the Hindu agitators gave an opportunity to the Muslim peasants to boycott the oppressive Hindu Zamindars and Marwari businessmen. The Muslim upper class countered the slogan of *Swadeshi* with that of *Swajati,* urging purely Muslim commerce, industry and education. Fuller's successor Hare reported genuine anti-Hindu feelings existing among the Muslims of Eastern Bengal and Assam.

In June 1906 Morley's announcement of forthcoming constitutional reforms in his budget speech in Parliament as well as his advice to Minto to immediately start talks on reform to prevent nationalist demands from getting stiffer, alarmed the Aligarh Muslims—a simple increase in the membership of the Legislative Councils of 1892 would tilt the balance greatly in favour of the Hindus. Mohsin-ul-Mulk, Secretary of the Aligarh College, expressed his fear to Principal Archibold, and requested him to arrange a Muslim deputation to Minto through his Private Secretary, Dunlop Smith. Minto immediately consented for he and some members of his Council saw an opportunity to alienate the young Aligarh Muslims who had passed a resolution in May 1906 advocating Hindu-Muslim political co-operation, from the Congress. Mohsin-ul-Mu!k told Archibold who drew up a formal request on behalf of the deputation on 4 August that a more active political line was necessary. He insisted on removing from Archibold's initial draft a sentence pledging "aloofness from political agitation" since the young Muslim radicals he wanted to counter were already saying "that the policy of Sir Syed and that of mine has done no good to Muhammedans."

Advised by Hare who was continuing Fuller's policy in fomenting Hindu-Muslim dissensions in the new province, Minto decided to receive the deputation at Simla on 10 October. The deputation was to consist not only of the Aligarh group but Muslims who had been opposed to the pro-British policy of Syed Ahmad. Its leader, Aga Khan, who had been rubbing shoulders with the Congress Moderates like Mehta and Tyabji since 1892 had been able to shed their influence as soon as he had visited Aligarh in 1906 and "had come to the conclusion that our only hope lay along the lines of independent organisation and action and that we must secure independent political recognition from the British Government as a nation within the nation."

Except for one item, the main arguments of the Muslim deputation had been mainly formulated by Archibold. While Archibold supported nomination, Bilgrami and Mohsin-ul-Mulk called for election on the basis of religion with an eye on the young radicals. They argued that they were a distinct community and did not like the idea of placing their interests at the mercy of "an unsympathetic majority" who would never back any but pro-Hindu Muslim—a clear demand for separate and communal electorate. They also demanded weightage besides their share of seats on numerical basis so that the Muslims could be an effective minority in the Punjab, Sind and Bengal. The separate Muslim electoral college would consist of landowners, lawyers, merchants, fellows and graduates of universities and members of district and local boards. Representatives of the peasantry and the lower middle class were not included.

While receiving the Muslim deputation "as a thoroughly representative body", Minto allayed the Muslim fear that the partition of Bengal would be undone. He assured them of safeguarding "their political rights and interests as a community by any administrative reorganization with which I am concerned." In a private conversation with Mohsin-ul-Mulk, he guaranteed him Muslim community representation in the projected reforms to combat growing Hindu influence.

Assured of their success, the Aga Khan was now shrewd enough to seize the occasion to institutionalize themselves in a political party. "I have asked", he wrote to Dunlop Smith, "all the Members of the Simla Deputation to form into a permanent committee." Nawab Mohsin-ul-Mulk was to be its Secretary and he was to obtain full approval of the British Raj before taking any move. The initiative was taken by Nawab Salimulla Khan of Dacca who circulated a letter containing a scheme for "the Muslim All-India Confederacy." The scheme was accepted with some modifications by a Muslim Conference at Dacca presided over by Viquar-ul-Mulk on 30 December 1906. The shorter name of the All-India Muslim League was adopted and Mohsin-ul-Mulk and Viquar-ul-Mulk were elected joint secretaries. The Muslim League was launched with the following objectives: "(1) to promote loyalty to the British Government, (2) to protect and advance the political rights and interests of Mussalmans of India and respectfully represent their needs and aspirations to Government and (3) to prevent, the rise among Mussalmans of any feelings towards other communities without prejudice to the other objects of the League." The last nine words of the third and final objective confirmed the first two objectives and revealed its real and true nature.

The birth of the Muslim League was the signal for aggravating the growing tensions between Hindus and Muslims in Eastern Bengal and Assam. The League declared the partition as beneficial to the Muslim interests and condemned the Anti-Partition Movement. The Muslims clashed with the *Swadeshi* agitators and the monster of communalism raised its hundred heads and showed its fangs in ugly riots particularly at Comilla and Jamalpur. The lot of the Muslim peasants was not certainly better than the lot of those belonging to the other community and Hare was worried that Bipin Chandra Pal might strengthen the unity of the two communities by exposing their common sufferings under the British rule. However, Nawab Salimullah Khan of Dacca himself held by the gold chain of a million pound loan provided by Curzon for his support of the Partition Plan was there to neutralize any such move by Pal. The dragon seeds of separatism sown by Syed Ahmad at Aligarh had now sprouted at Simla.

Chapter 16

Surat Split

In the last quarter of 1906 when the Muslim League was about to sprout at Simla, the Moderate Congress leaders were worried over the possible election of an Extremist as the President of the forthcoming Congress session in Calcutta. In the 1905 Benares Congress the Moderates were almost compelled to give a qualified support to the boycott and *Swadeshi* programme by a threat of opposition from the Extremists to a Moderate resolution welcoming the forthcoming visit to India of the Prince and Princess of Wales "most humbly and respectfully." The Extremist challenge at the Benares Congress in December 1905 was indeed a weak one but over the next few months as Fuller went on taking measure after harsh measure against popular liberties, insulting highly esteemed leaders like Aswini Kumar Dutta, banning student participation in *Swadeshi* meetings and singing of *Bande Mataram* and quartering military and punitive force on Barisal, it grew in strength with a vigorous drive towards *Swadeshi* and boycott in preparation for the first anniversary of the partition. The Extremists now began to canvass for Tilak's election to the presidency of the next Congress.

Gokhale who had observed the weakness of the Moderate faction at the Benares Congress felt that the only way to arrest the ascendancy of the Extremists was to obtain the annulment of the partition by peaceful means and a promise of colonial self-government from the British Cabinet. On his ability and luck depended the position of the Moderates and he went to England to wheedle out of the Liberal Secretary of State, Morley, the twin objects. Having analysed the revolutionary psychology of the French Revolution and the Irish Anarchism as a student, Morley, the biographer of Gladstone, quickly grasped the Moderate impasse and wondered "whether by doing what we can in the Moderate direction, we can draw the teeth of the Extremists." After a series of fairly fruitful meetings with Gokhale, Morley announced the forthcoming constitutional reforms in his budget speech and asked Minto in June 1906 to balance the maintenance of the unpopular partition with some reforms—some more Indians for the Legislative, and perhaps, Executive Councils, more time for budget discussions and permission for amendments. Minto also realised that "friendly recognition of a Moderate Congress" would "do much good. If the extremists such as Tilak and B.C. Pal, gain the ascendancy, it will be impossible to deal with them, and the Congress itself will split up." As a matter of fact, Tilak's growing ascendancy in the Congress not only worried Morley and Minto but also the Bombay Moderates like Dinshaw Wacha and Pherozeshah Mehta, who threatened, as Gokhale was informed by Wedderburn on 8 August 1906, that if Lajpat or Tilak were elected President, "Bombay will reconsider its position— meaning, apparently, withdrawal from the Congress." Gokhale was particularly alarmed that such an event would certainly adversely affect Morley's sympathetic views on reforms. The Moderates ultimately had recourse to subterfuge and they skilfully manoeuvred Dadabhai Naoroji, then 82 years old, to the presidential chair at the Calcutta session. The Extremists had the good sense to yield to the father-figure but behind the scenes dissension ran rife.

It was for the first time in the Congress Movement that Naoroji defined in his presidential address at the Calcutta session the goal of the Congress as "self-government or Swaraj like that of the United Kingdom or the colonies." The Calcutta Congress marked the climax of the extremist influence over the Congress with its resolutions on Boycott, *Swadeshi,* National Education and Self-Government or Swaraj. Bipin Chandra Pal's attempt to extend boycott to other provinces and honorary offices besides foreign goods was repudiated by Malaviya and the issue was clinched by Gokhale who pointed out that they were bound by the words of all the four resolutions which were subject to different interpretations. For example, what was innocuous "Swaraj" to Gokhale was 'Swarajya" to Tilak, which in every Marathi ear sounded like the battle cry of Shivaji.

Communal tensions let loose by the Muslim League in Eastern Bengal and Assam and a reign of terror let loose by the British policy of repression contributed further to the extremist movement when Tilak and Pal gave a call for passive resistance to the British rule at the utmost personal sacrifice. "The point is to have the entire control in our hands", declared Tilak on 2 January 1907. Pal's activities in the new province led Banerjea, "the king of Bengal", as described by Minto to Morley in his letter on 9 March 1907, to meet Minto for his "assistance to moderate the evil passions of the Bengalis." Banerjea was followed by Gokhale who met Minto to inform him that "the whole younger generation of India is going over to the extremists' side and that the only way to recover our moral control is to do something that will appeal to the native imagination." The lure of the forthcoming constitutional reforms and the increasing popularity of the extremist activities all over India brought the Moderate leaders closer to the British Raj and further widened the gulf between them and the Extremist leaders.

An indication of this was provided by the Bombay Provincial Conference held at Surat in April 1907 where the Mehta group were successful in excluding the Calcutta Congress resolutions on Boycott and National Education from the Conference programme. In the Bengal Provincial Conference at Midnapore rowdyism broke out on account of differences between the Moderates and the

Extremists, particularly on account of the refusal of the Moderate Chairman to discuss Swaraj and the police had to be called in to restore order. Things moved further to a Congress split when Lajpat Rai was deported and Tilak gave a call for retaliation in a *Kesari* article on 21 May 1907: "If the rulers adopt this Russian method, then the subjects in India will have to imitate the subjects of Russia." Gokhale felt that the deportation of Lajpat,—"with my intimate knowledge of the man, his work and his methods",—had nullified all the good efforts of Morley's budget speech promising reforms and anticipated a split in the Congress soon.

In October 1907 Gokhale actually wrote to Morley to know "how the split in Congress, now apparently inevitable, is to be averted." Morley thought that Gokhale was "a baby as a party manager." A party manager should never whine but Gokhale was always whining. "Now, if I were in Gokhale's shoes—if he wears shoes, I forget," wrote Morley to Minto on 31 October 1907, "I should insist on quietly making terms with the bureaucracy on the basis of Order plus Reforms. If he would have the sense to see what is to be gained by this time, the "Split" when it comes should do him no harm, because it would set him free to fix his aims on reasonable things, where he might get out of us sixty or seventy percent of what he might ask for."

The formal split was now a question of time. Mehta managed to shift the venue of the forthcoming session of the Congress from Nagpur which was Tilak's stronghold to his own stronghold at Surat and thus ensured the election of a very Moderate leader, Rashbehari Ghosh as President in place of Lajpat Rai whose name had been proposed by the Extremists after his release from deportation. The list of agenda at the Surat Congress officially announced 10 days before the session did not include the subjects of self-government, boycott and national education. Tilak who came to Surat on 23 December denounced this retrograde step and decided to frustrate it at any cost unless he was given an assurance that the Calcutta Congress resolutions on these subjects would not be modified in any way at Surat. Having failed to elicit this assurance from the Moderates, Tilak and his group opposed the election to Rashbehari Ghosh as President of the Surat Congress on 26 December and the Reception Committee Chairman, Malvi, suspended the meeting amidst uproarious scenes. On 27 December Tilak's move for an adjournment motion was ruled out by Malvi and when Ghosh tried to read his presidential address, Tilak kept shouting that he must move his motion. An attempt to lift Tilak bodily out of the meeting was resisted by Tilak's followers who had actually come prepared with sticks and in the melee that followed, a Marathi *chappal* struck both Mehta and Banerjea on the platform. The President adjourned the Congress *sine die.* Next day Tilak's attempt at a compromise was scuttled by the Moderates who held their convention on 29 December. The Extremists were not allowed to join it. The Convention appointed a committee consisting of nearly hundred persons to provide the Congress with a constitution which was to later describe the Congress methods as "strictly constitutional" limited to bringing about "steady reform of the existing system of administration" and to restrict delegate election to "recognised bodies of over three years' standing" thereby deliberately keeping the future sessions of the Congress closed to the Extremists. The Congress of 1885 had now definitely split at Surat in December 1907.

Chapter 17

Act of 1909

The constitutional reforms on which the Moderates pinned the hopes in their showdown with the Extremists in the Surat Congress of 1907 took a further two years to materialise in the Government of India Act of 1909. An inkling of the reforms which provided the basis for this Act was given by Morley when he wrote to Minto in June 1906 informing him that "cast-iron bureaucracy won't go on forever" though he did not visualise the introduction of English political institutions into India— "Assuredly not in your days or mine".

The Act did not introduce any changes in the executive sphere. One seat on the Viceroy's Executive Council was, in actual practice, reserved for an Indian member and the number of Executive Councilors in Bombay and Madras was increased from three to four, the way thus being left open for the appointment of a non-official. An Executive Council was created in Bengal, and provision made for the creation of such Councils elsewhere on certain conditions. Despite the fact that the Act of 1909 did not specially provide for the appointment of Indians on Provincial Executive Councils, the practice was begun of including such members in them with the appointment of Raja Kishori Lal Goswami as a member of the Executive Council of Bengal.

It was in the composition and functions of the Legislative Council that the Act introduced important changes. The number of additional members of the Central Legislature was raised from 16 to a maximum of 60, of whom not more than 28 were to be officials. The Viceroy was given the power to nominate five members including three non-officials to represent certain specified communities. The remaining 27 seats were to be filled by non-official elected members, some of whom represented certain special constituencies such as the landowners in seven provinces, the Muslims in five provinces, and two Chambers of Commerce in Calcutta and Bombay, while the rest (13) were to be elected by the non-official members of the nine Provincial Legislative Councils. A small official majority was thus retained in the Central Legislature.

In the Provincial Legislature, the number of additional members was raised to a maximum of fifty in the major provinces in such a way that a combination of official and nominated non-official members might have a small majority over the elected members, except in Bengal where there was a clear elected majority. The major part of these additional non-official members were to be elected by groups of local bodies, landholders, trade associations and universities. The Government of India was given power to disqualify any one of these members as politically dangerous. By conceding the demand of the Muslim community of separate representation by members chosen by the votes of a Muslim electorate, the Act of 1909 introduced the principle of communal representation which was to become "a cardinal problem and ground of controversy at every revision of the Indian electoral system." And the shadow of Pakistan loomed large on the horizon.

The Act of 1909 empowered the Legislature to discuss, and to move resolutions on, the Budget, before it was finally settled, and certain matters of general interest excluding Army, Foreign Relations and the Indian States, which, however, could be disallowed by the Head of the Government acting as President of the Council at his discretion.

The hopes of the Moderates raised by Morley's announcement of constitutional reforms in June 1906 and sustained since that year in the Moderates' hearts were now dashed to the ground. The official majority at the Centre and the hoax of the non-official majorities in the provinces, the arbitrary powers of disqualification, the narrow franchise and the principle of communal representation, the restriction on debates and the limited power of influencing the budget disillusioned them. The Moderates could act now only as a sterile opposition as nothing that they might say could lead to any modification in the fundamental policy of the government which continued to be carried on with absolute responsibility to White Hall. The Moderates who had welcomed the reform proposals of Morley as "large and liberal" at the Madras Congress in December 1908 now felt cheated by Morley who denied that the reforms had ever been meant to introduce English political institutions in India. As he observed in the House of Lords on 17 December 1908 during debates on these reforms: "If it could be said that this chapter of reforms led directly or indirectly to the establishment of a parliamentary system in India, I, for one, would have nothing at all to do with it." It was clear the Act had now made the task of organising a national movement uniting all the people of India irrespective of their caste, creed or religion more difficult by its principle of communal electorates.

The discomfiture of the Moderates now spelt success for the Extremists. Many Congressmen increasingly became dissatisfied with the approach of their Moderate leaders who were now fiercely attacked by the Extremists. Hardinge who succeeded Minto tried to stem the tide of rising nationalism by repealing the partition of Bengal in December 1911. Bihar and Orissa were taken out of Bengal and Assam was created a separate province. The capital was also shifted from Calcutta to a safer place in Delhi where, in December 1912, the Viceroy was greeted with a Bengal bomb which narrowly missed his life.

Chapter 18

Revolutionaries At Home and Abroad

The bomb attack on Hardinge on 23 December 1912 when he was making his official entry into the new Capital was planned by Rashbehari Bose and Schindranath Sanyal who knit together a far-flung secret organisation with centres in the Punjab, Delhi and the United Provinces. Since 1911 the Dacca *Anushilan Samiti* of Pulinbehari Das had concentrated on raising funds through *Swadeshi* dacoities and assassinating British officials while the Yugantar Party led by Jatindranath Mukherjee had started building international contacts so that a real military assault could be organised against the British Raj. These young revolutionaries had no faith in the laborious and prolonged constitutional agitation of the Congress. Fired with a fiery love for their motherland and disgusted with a bitter hatred against the British Raj, they wanted freedom not only for their children but for themselves by more violent and direct means.

Many of these revolutionaries by 1911 had escaped British Raj's grasp by taking shelter abroad where they could bring out revolutionary journals free from the jurisdiction of the Newspapers Act of 1908, which had gagged the radical weeklies, *Bande Mataram, Sandhya* and *Yugantar* in India and develop contacts for supplying arms and ammunition to the revolutionaries in India. Still many among them were sent abroad by revolutionary organisations in India with a plan to organise centres in Europe,

U.S.A., the Middle East and South-East Asia where the cause of India could be propagated and arms and money collected to further revolution at home. The fresh recruits to the centres that they set up came mostly from young Indian students, businessmen and emigrant workers. When the First World War broke out in 1914, they planned to supply the Indian revolutionary organisations with recruits, funds and arms.

One of the earliest among such revolutionary centres abroad was the one set up by Shyamji Krishnavarma in London in 1905. He brought out a journal, *Indian Sociologist,* organised an Indian Home Rule Society and instituted a scholarship scheme to bring radical students from India. From 1907 onwards Shyamji's centre India House, came to be dominated by a revolutionary group led by V.D. Savarkar from Nasik, and in July 1908 one member of this group, Madanlal Dhingra, assassinated the India Office bureaucrat, Curzon Wyllie. Dhingra went to the scaffold with these words on his lips: "Neither rich nor able, a poor son like myself can offer nothing but his blood on the altar of his Mother's deliverance. May I be reborn of the same mother and may I redie in the same sacred cause, till my mission is done and she stands free for the good of humanity and to the glory of God." In 1910 Savarkar was extradited to be given life transportation in the Nasik Conspiracy Case and with this, the London revolutionaries dispersed. An associate of Savarkar, Madame Cama, a Parsi revolutionary, went to Geneva, developed close contacts with Paris based Socialists like Jean Longuet and brought out a revolutionary paper, *Bande Mataram.* Another associate, Virendranath Chattopadhyaya first went to Paris and then to Germany where he resumed his revolutionary activities. When the First World War broke out, he became the Secretary of the Indian Independence Committee which was formed in Berlin in 1915 with German Foreign Office subsidy. The Committee sent missions to Baghdad, Istanbul, and Persia to work among Indian army units and Indian prisoners of war. And in December 1915 Raja Mahendra Pratap was sent to Kabul with Maulana Barkataullah and Maulana Obeidullah Sindhi, where they formed a "Provisional Government of Free India" with some active backing from the Crown Prince Amanullah.

One year before the war broke out the Ghadr Movement was started in 1913 in San Francisco by Sohan Singh Bhakna, Taraknath Das and Har Dayal among a colony of fairly prosperous Indian traders and workers, mostly from the Punjab, in British Columbia and the Pacific Coast States of the United States, who were embittered by the strict American Immigration Laws, about which the British Raj had not done anything to improve their position. The Ghadr Party, took its name from a weekly paper, *Ghadr,* brought out from 1 November 1913 in Urdu, and Gurmukhi, in commemoration of the Revolt of 1857, which began its first issue with this dramatic observation: "What is our name. The *Ghadr* (Revolution). In what does our work consist? In bringing about a rising. Where will the rising break out? In India. When will it break out ? In a few years."

The outbreak of the First World War provided the Ghadrites with an opportunity to free India. They began to return to India in their thousands. They got in touch with Rashbehari Bose and Sachindranath Sanyal who had earlier staged the unsuccessful bomb attack on Hardinge to organise a far-flung conspiracy to drive the British out of India. Their passions were further inflamed by the Komagata Maru incident on 29 September 1914 when a ship load of Sikh and Muslim immigrants from the Punjab, turned back by the Canadian immigration authorities from Vancouver, clashed with the police on their return at Budge Budge near Calcutta. Twenty-two of them were killed while many were injured and the news led the Punjabis abroad to hasten back to India to fight the British Raj. However, their plan for co-ordinated revolt in collaboration with the Bengal revolutionaries on 21 February 1915 based on mutinies by the Indian garrisons at Ferozepur, Lahore, Rawalpindi, Meerat, Benares and Danapur was foiled at the last moment by treachery. Rashbehari Bose fled to Japan, Sachindranath Sanyal was transported for life and among the 47 lowly placed Ghadr peasants and the sepoy heroes who were executed was Kartar Singh Sarabha, 19 year old organiser of mutiny among the Punjab garrisons, who died with these words: "If I had to live more lives than one, I would sacrifice each of them for my country's sake."

The Bengal revolutionaries Rashbehari Bose who fled to Japan and Sanyal who was transported for life were part of a wider group of revolutionaries which had united under the Yugantar party led by Jatindranath Mukherjee, nicknamed "Bagha Jatin," for his unique courage, deeds and fighting qualities. The Bengal revolutionaries appropriated a large consignment of 50 Mouser pistols and 46,000 rounds of ammunition from Rodda and Company through a sympathetic employee in August 1914. "Bagha Jatin" planned an armed rebellion after the failure of the co-ordinated still-born revolt on 21 February 1915 with the help of arms and ammunitions imported from Germany and Naren Bhattacharji who later became famous as M.N. Roy, was sent to Java to arrange safe landing of German arms in India. The police got scent of the grandiose plan. A memorable battle look place on 9 September 1915 between a battalion of armed police and five Bengali revolutionaries waiting to unload German arms on the banks of the Buribalam river at Balasore. Jatindranath courted death valiantly while putting up a gallant fight. The plan of an armed rising with German help thus failed.

The revolutionaries failed because of a lack of co-ordination among the revolutionary leaders in India as well as a lack of communication between them and the Committee in Berlin and the Ghadr Party in San Francisco. The British Raj persuaded the United States to foil shipment of arms to the revolutionaries in India and after the United States joined the Allies in the war against Germany, any further revolutionary activities there became quite difficult. In India the Raj passed the Defence of India Act in March

1915 after the detection of an armed conspiracy in February to meet the threats posed by the revolutionaries. Large number of suspects were held without trial for years in Bengal and the Punjab, and extremely severe sentences were handed down by special courts set up within the provisions of the Defence of India Act to those found guilty.

Chapter 19

Lucknow Pact

Within a year after the failure of the revolutionaries at home and abroad to achieve freedom of their motherland, significant developments took place concerning the Indian National Congress which had splitted at Surat in 1907. As we have already said the Indian Councils Act of 1909 left the Moderates unhappy with the British Raj. An important section of the Moderates started not only to drift away from the Raj but to think in terms of somewhat greater militancy. Attendance at the annual Congress sessions began to fall off sharply though on the floor of the reformed Central Legislative Council, Gokhale made his mark as an eloquent orator and debater, arguing the case of universal primary education, attacking repressive policies of the Raj, and drawing public attention to Indians in South Africa. These were also the issues which agitated the Moderates at the annual Congress sessions which became, without the presence of the Extremists, "very dull," as Jawaharlal Nehru wrote in his *Autobiography.*

Tilak was released from his Mandaley exile in 1914 with the outbreak of the First World War which offered to him an opportunity to work with a renewed vigour and vitality. He was keen to make up with his old Congress enemies. Except Gokhale and Mehta, other Moderate leaders were quite willing to accept Tilak and Bhupendranath Bose in particular, suggested to Gokhale on 26 November 1914 to "accept any means to lift the Congress out of the present bog." However, what helped Tilak to move closer to the Congress was the sudden rise to political prominence in 1914 of the Theosophist leader, Annie Besant who had come to realise that a large measure of self-government was imperative for Indo-British friendship and the only means of achieving this object was through effective national agitation and organisation modelled on the British Radical and Irish Home Rule Movements. Tilak now joined hands with Besant. The death of Gokhale, the wisest and ablest of the Moderates at an early age of fortynine, in February 1915, left the Congress without an effective leadership. Mehta who had proved obdurate to Tilak's rejoining the Congress also died towards the end of 1915. And Annie Besant had little difficulty in persuading the Congress to allow the Tilak group to rejoin its session in Bombay in December 1915. The Muslim League also held its session in Bombay in December 1915. Both the Congress and the League set up committees to draft a platform of minimum constitutional demands through mutual consultation.

The League came closer to the Congress because of the important developments that had affected its fortune in the immediate pre-war years. In December 1911 George V who as the Prince of Wales in 1905-06 had seen something of the Bengal agitation at first hand, announced the revocation of the partition at the Delhi Durbar as a royal boon and both Hardinge and Crew, the Secretary of State, found that this royal boon was less expensive than the other boons suggested by the King, which was strongly endorsed by the Home Member Jenkins: "Until we get rid of the partition ulcer, we shall have no peace." So the new province of Eastern Bengal and Assam which had undoubtedly benefited the Muslim elite there was wound up in December 1911 amidst loud protests of the Muslim League. The transfer of the Capital from Calcutta to the seat of Muslim glory in Delhi failed to mollify the wounded sentiments of the Muslims in British India. Secondly, Britain's refusal to help Turkey, the seat of the Caliphate, in her Italian and Balkan Wars during 1911-12 and Hardinge's rejection of proposals for a Muslim university at Aligarh in August 1912 had further alienated them from the British Raj. And finally, great changes had taken place within the Muslim League itself since it had been captured in 1912 by young leaders like Wazir Hassan, T.A.K. Sherwani, Muhammad and Shaukat Ali, Hasrat Mohani of the United Provinces, Zafar Ali Khan of the Punjab and Fazlul Huq of Bengal. They steered the League towards greater militancy, some kind of accommodation with nationalist Hindus and increasing Pan-Islamism which was revealed in their growing concern for Turkey when they sent in 1912-13 a medical mission led by Ansari and Zafar Ali Khan to help Turkey in the Balkan War. In March 1913 Wazir Hassan as the new Secretary of the Muslim League pushed through and successfully carried a resolution which stated that colonial self-government through constitutional means was to be the aim of the League. This brought the League in tune with the Moderate Congress.

With Tilak's realisation that success against the British Raj could be achieved only through Hindu-Muslim unity, the stage was set for a period of general Hindu-Muslim political co-operation. In December 1916 both the Congress and the League held their sessions at Lucknow. Here an alliance was concluded between them which became famous as the Lucknow Pact. A joint scheme of constitutional advance on the basis of Dominion Status was adopted. The Congress accepted the League demand for "separate electorates". The League accepted Congress suggestion for under-representation in Muslim majority areas like Bengal in return for over-representation in provinces like Bombay or the United Provinces. The Pact which clearly reflected the interests of the U.P. based young party of Wazir Hassan and Mabmudabad aroused some resentment among Muslims in Bengal despite the support provided by the Fazlul Huq group to it.

The Pact was, no doubt, a Congress "surrender to Moslems" but the sight of the League and the Congress marching together for a common cause not only alarmed the British Raj but raised high expectations among the nationalists in India. The Muslim League though prompted by their concern for Turkey and the Caliphate, had nevertheless overcome to a great extent the fears deeply planted by the Aligarh Movement. Looked at from this point of view, the Pact was "a triumph for Indian nationalism" though ultimately it failed to stand the test of time as it was based upon the pernicious and wrong ideas that Hindus and Muslims formed two separate communities in India.

Chapter 20

Home Rule

The Lucknow Congress of December 1916 ruled out Tilak's proposal to set up a Working Committee as a first step towards transforming the Congress from a deliberative body of annually passing pious resolutions into a real party. It was through the two Home Rule Leagues one set up by Tilak in April 1916 and the other by Besant in September 1916 that agitational work had to be organised.

Annie Besant, with her "Irish blood and Irish heart," was responsible for introducing Home Rule Movement in India. Besant came to India in 1893 as a Theosophist. And as President of the Theosophical Society in India, since 1907, devoted herself to the social and educational upliftment of the Indians. However, she soon came to realise that no real improvement was possible without raising the political status of India. In early 1914 she went to England to rouse English public opinion in favour of the Indian demand for self-government. She failed in her attempt to form an Indian Party in the British Parliament but succeeded in setting up a Home Rule League in London. On her return to India she bought a daily paper in Madras, renamed it *New India* which she published on 14 July, the day of the fall of the Bastille. It was in this paper on 25 September 1915 that she made a formal announcement about the Home Rule League and moved a resolution on it in the Bombay Congress in December 1915 which was ruled out by the Congress as it contravened Article 1 of the Congress Constitution which limited the scope of the demand for self-government by such words as "bringing about a steady reform of the existing system of administration." It was, however agreed that a paper on the subject of Home Rule, would be prepared by the Congress Committee for consideration before 1 September 1916.

Tilak was, however, free from any such constraints on his return from Mandaley in 1914 and before rejoining the Congress in December 1915, he summoned a conference of the nationalists at Poona to discuss the desirability of establishing a League to obtain Home Rule for India. On the basis of a report submitted by a committee appointed for the purpose at the Poona Conference, the Belgaum Conference of April 1916 resolved to establish the Indian Home Rule League "to attain Home Rule or Self-Government within the British Empire by all constitutional means and to educate and organise public opinion in the country towards the attainment of the same." In a leading article in the *Mahratta*, Tilak justified the formation of the League as "the Congress is too unwieldly to be easily moved to prepare a scheme for self-government and actively work for its practical success. The spade work has got to be done by someone. It can afford to wait no longer." In stirring articles in the *Mahratta* and the *Kesari* Tilak argued that Home Rule for India should be demanded without waiting for the termination of the war. He asked for a time limit to be laid down in a Parliamentary Bill within which India should be given full self-government. "All [Ireland, for example] are demanding Swaraj now," he said, "and the British can no longer resist the demand [for India]." He undertook an extensive lecture tour by the middle of 1916, for instructing masses on Home Rule and exhorting them to become members of the League. Tilak's homely speeches and his direct appeal to the masses made him not only popular but a hero among them. The impact of Tilak's tour could be seen when he went to attend the Congress at Lucknow, the tyres of his car were deflated to force the Reception

Committee to put him in a carriage which was unhorsed and dragged through the streets amidst the wild acclamation of a huge procession. Tilak's intense patriotism, selfness service for the cause of nationalism and bold leadership earned for him the affectionate honorific, *Loka Manya.*

By 1 September 1916, the Congress having failed to produce a draft Home Rule Scheme, Besant felt free to organise a regular Home Rule League in September 1916 and set up within a few days, branches at Bombay, Kanpur, Allahabad, Benares, Mathura, Calicut and Ahmadnagar. She now began an active propaganda through lectures and her two press organs, *New India* and *Commonwealth*. She took full advantage of the existing organisation of the Theosophical Society as well as of the personal devotion and admiration felt for her intellect, learning and religious mission by a wide circle of Indians.

The two Home Rule Leagues worked in close co-operation with each other. After the Lucknow Congress, Tilak and Besant visited many parts of India, which were described in police reports as "triumphant tours" and addressed largely attended public meetings. The movement spread like wild fire and among the many young men activized by it were numerous future leaders of Indian politics from the 1920 onwards including Jawaharlal Nehru, Satyamurti and Indulal Yajnik. One interesting feature of the movement was an increasing participation in it by the women. As Besant declared: "Our League's best recruits and recruiters are among the women of India, and the women of Madras boast that they marched in procession when the men were stopped and that their prayers in the temples set the interned captives free."

The success of the movement created great concern among the British authorities in India. "The position is of great difficulty," observed the Home Member confidentially in January 1917. "Moderate leaders can command no support among the vocal class who are being led at the heels of Tilak and Besant." In May 1917 Tilak held the annual conference of his League at Nasik and emphasised that the League, unlike the Congress, was pledged to work zealously throughout the year for the sole object of achieving Home Rule. He would be glad to dissolve the League in two years, after the grant of Home Rule to India. After the Nasik Conference, the Leaguers redoubled their efforts to carry the Home Rule propaganda to the villages. "Mrs. Besant, Tilak and others are fomenting with great vigour the agitation for immediate Home Rule," Chelmsford informed Montagu, the Secretary of State, "and in the absence of any definite announcement by Government of India as to their policy in the matter, it is attracting many of those who hitherto have held less advanced views."

The Raj's reaction began with the internment of Besant and two of her associates, Arundale and Wadia. While in Britain the action was adversely criticised, a storm of indignation blew in India from one end to the other. Under Tilak's guidance, the Congress Committee made a vigorous protest to the Viceroy and asked for the release of Besant and her associates and also decided to elect Besant as President of the Congress session in December 1917. In July 1917 the Congress Committee held a joint meeting with the Council of the League at Madras to consider the question of adopting passive resistance to protest against the repressive policy of the government and secure the release of Besant and her associates.

It was in this circumstance that Edwin Montagu made his historic pronouncement on reforms on 20 August 1917 in the House of Commons: "The policy of His Majesty's Government with which the Government of India are in complete accord is that of the increasing association of Indians in every branch of the administration and the gradual development of self-governing institutions with a view to the progressive realisation of responsible government in India as an integral part of the British Empire." The announcement was followed by the release of the Home Rule prisoners including Besant. At this the Congress Committee and the League Council met again at Allahabad in October 1917 to drop the question of passive resistance much to the disappointment of the younger section and decided to send a deputation to the Raj in support of the Congress-League scheme of self-government. Montagu who came to India to discuss the practical aspects of his reform proposals met Tilak on 27 November and unsuccessfully tried to secure his support for them.

Attended by nearly five thousand delegates including four hundred ladies, the Congress held its session in December 1917 at Calcutta, with Tilak's nominee, Besant, as its President. Besant, in her eloquent address, made a vigorous plea for immediate introduction of a Bill in the British Parliament for the establishment of self-government in India, preferably in 1923 and not later than 1928. An official confidential report commented, "The capture of the Congress organization by Mrs. Besant and Tilak is complete. The Moderate party in the Congress is extinguished. The Congress is completely identified with Home Rule."

In April 1918 after Montagu's return to London, the British Raj published the report on Indian constitutional reforms which sought to tackle the problems of realizing "responsible government" by provincial autonomy and the peculiar device of "diarchy", transferring certain functions of provincial government like education, health, agriculture, local bodies to ministers responsible to Legislative assemblies while keeping other subjects "reserved". The publication of the report dashed to the ground the great expectations raised by Montagu's announcement of 20 August 1917. While the Moderates welcomed the report as a definite advancement to the realisation of self-government in India, the Extremists rejected it totally. In a special session held in Bombay in August 1918, the Congress reiterated the demand for self-government, condemned the report as inadequate, disappointing and unsatisfactory, and passed a number of resolution proposing modifications. The Moderates boycotted the session, and many of them like Banerjea, Chintamoni, Sapru and Jayakar left the Congress to later found the National Liberal Federation of India.

Henceforward the Indian National Congress became, as shrewdly prophesied by Morley after the first split at Surat in 1907, "an Extremist organization."

With Besant becoming almost overnight a pro-Raj supporter after Montagu's promise of "responsible government" in India and Tilak becoming increasingly involved in a libel suit against Valentine Chirol in England, the Home Rule Movement, with its offices at New York and London, was mainly carried on by a new generation of young leaders in India. The Home Rule Movement penetrated new areas and attracted new groups. Har Dayal wrote from Stockholm: "I have become an adherent of the party of Home Rule in India instead of the old Revolutionary Party which aimed at the dissolution of the British Empire in India." Unlike the Congress, the Home Rule Movement was not an annual political affair—but a whole time pre-occupation throughout the year for the attainment of self-government in India. Its message was carried to the masses in clear simple language by Tilak and Besant and by the end of 1918 the ground was thus prepared for the emergence of a new leader who was to dominate the Indian political scene for the next thirty years.

Section III
The Climactic Years, 1918-1947

Chapter 21

Rowlatt Act

In 1917 when at the height of the Home Rule Movement Montagu announced his reform proposals in the British Parliament to rally the Moderates, Chelmsford in India appointed a committee consisting of four persons under Justice Rowlatt of England to recommend legislation for suppression of the revolutionary movement against the British Raj. The Committee's recommendations were eventually based on the draft Bill of the Government of India to replace the Defence of India Act which would cease to be operative after the end of the war and two Bills were prepared out of these. The one that was actually passed into law, the Anarchical and Revolutionary Crimes Act, 1919, which provided for speedy trial of offences without any appeal, gave wide powers to the provincial governments to search a place and arrest a suspected person without warrant and keep him in confinement in such place and under such conditions as they might specify. Despite strenuous opposition from the non-official Indian members, the Central Legislative Council passed it on 18 March and put it in the Statute Book on 21 March 1919. While the Act remained practically a dead letter, it brought into lime light Mohandas Karam Chand Gandhi — a new leader with a new technique.

Gandhi had first attracted attention by his successful application of *Satyagraha* for vindicating the rights of Indians in South Africa.

He originally described his movement in South Africa as "Passive Resistance" but in 1907 he deliberately substituted the term, *Satyagraha* for it, partly because he was ashamed to use an English word and partly because he wanted to emphasise an essential difference between his movement and the Passive Resistance. As he himself put it: "*Satyagraha* differs from Passive Resistance as the North Pole from the South. The latter has been conceived as a weapon of the weak and does not exclude the use of physical force or violence for the purpose of gaining one's end; whereas the former has been conceived as a weapon of the strongest, and excludes the use of violence in any shape and form." *Satyagraha* in South Africa where he went as a lawyer of a firm of Porbandar Muslims in May 1893 involved after 1906 careful training of disciplined cadres, peaceful violation of specific laws like compulsory registration, entry permits and trade licenses, mass courting of arrests, and occasional hartals and spectacular marches. It also included a combination of apparently quixotic methods together with meticulous attention to organisational matters, a readiness for negotiations and compromise, at times leading to abrupt unilateral withdrawals which were by no means popular and the cultivation of what non-disciples usually considered to be the Gandhian fads like vegetarianism, nature-therapy and sexual self-restraint. While this programme of Satyagraha was able to attract the masses, it also helped to keep mass activity anchored to certain forms pre-determined by the leader, and above all, to the methods of non-violence. Gandhi's experience of working in South Africa among a people of different religions, communities, castes and classes—Hindus, Muslims, Parsis and Christians, Gujaratis and South Indians, upper-class merchants and lawyers as well as Newcastles mine workers whom Gandhi led in a memorable strike and cross-country march in October 1913 helped him to emerge more easily as a potential all-India figure than any other politician, all of whom like Banerjea, Mehta, Gokhale, Tilak, Lajpat or Pal, had essentially regional bases and interests.

In 1915 Gandhi returned from South Africa after having won a partial victory against Smut's regime and set up an *Ashram* at Ahmedabad on the banks of the Sabarmati to teach Indians the ideals and methods of Satyagraha. In the next three years that followed Gandhi acquired the reputation of a political leader who would take up local wrongs and work among the local masses, a political style in sharp contrast to the established Congress and League method of starting with somewhat abstract all-India programmes and then proceeding from top downwards. Thus in April 1917 he led a successful movement which put an end to the oppression of the indigo planters on the peasants of Champaran in North Bihar. His recourse to the first of his many historic fasts led to a satisfactory settlement of a long-drawn dispute between Ahmedabad mill owners and their workers. And finally his advice to the cultivators at Kheda to resort to *Satyagraha* bore fruit when all attempts to settle their claim to a suspension of the revenue assessment were in vain following the failure of the crops at Kheda.

Gandhi now appealed to Chelmsford for a repeal of the Rowlatt Bills and offered to *Satyagraha* if the Bills were passed by the Central Legislative Council. On 24 February 1917 he called a small meeting of about twenty persons including Vallabhbhai Patel and Sarojini Naidu, who took the *Satyagraha* pledge drafted by Gandhi: "We solemnly affirm that in the event of these Bills becoming law and until they are withdrawn, we shall refuse civilly to obey these laws and such other laws as a committee to be hereafter appointed, may think fit, and we further affirm that in this struggle, we will faithfully follow truth and refrain from violence to life, person or property." A *Satyagraha Sabha* was established, with Gandhi as its President and headquarters at Bombay, which issued bulletins and organised public meetings to attract signatories to the *Satyagraha* pledge. As one of the Bills was passed into a law on 21 March, Gandhi proposed that the country should observe a general hartal. All the people should suspend business for a day and observe it as one of fasting and prayer as a fitting preliminary to *Satyagraha,* an idea which was welcomed by many Congress leaders including Rajagopalachari and Gandhi drafted a brief appeal to the people. The day of hartal was fixed on 30 March but was subsequently changed to 6 April.

This novel method of agitation appealed to many younger members of the Home Rule Leagues who had been, since the conversion of Besant into a Moderate leader and the departure of Tilak in September 1918 for England, left without a dynamic leader. As Nehru wrote in his *Autobiography,* the first reaction of the young nationalists was "one of tremendous relief, a way out of the tangle, a method of action which was straight and open and possibly effective." It also appealed to the young radicals of the Muslim League who had captured power in the December 1918 session at Delhi. In this session Gandhi who had developed good relations with them was hailed by one of them, Ansari, as "the intrepid leader of India who has endeared himself as much to the Mussalmans as to the Hindus." And in mid-March Abodul Bari and his Firangi Mahal Ulema group of Lucknow came out in favour of *Satyagraha* against the Rowlatt Act after a meeting with Gandhi.

What followed on 30 March at Delhi, among others where the change of date reached too late and on 6 April at Calcutta, Bombay, Ahmedabad, Amritsar, Lahore and many smaller towns all over India was an upsurge against the British Raj—perhaps the biggest since 1857—sparked off by post-war economic grievances including rising prices, rumours, including arrest and assault, about Gandhi that were potent precisely in their vagueness and inaccuracy, and finally brutal provocation and repression, particularly in the Punjab following the Ghadr outbreak in 1915. Michael O'Dwyer's Punjab administration was frightened by the remarkable Hindu-Muslim-Sikh unity displayed by the people in a province noted for communal divisions. On 30 March and 6 April the hartals at Amritsar passed off peacefully but on 9 April when the *Ram Navami* procession, largely participated by Muslims, demonstrated spectacular scenes of "people of the different creeds drinking out of the same cups publicly," O' Dwyer swiftly swung into action the same evening issuing orders deporting the local leaders of Amritsar, Kitchlew and Satyapal, and restraining Gandhi from entering Delhi and the Punjab. People attacked banks, post offices, the railway stations, and the town hall—all symbols of British authority,—following firing on a peaceful demonstration at Hall Bridge in Amritsar on 10 April and the next day martial law under General Dyer was clamped on the town. And on 13 April at an enclosed ground, Jallianwallabag, a peaceful unarmed crowd, consisting mostly of villagers who had come for a fair and had not been told of the ban on meetings under martial law were gunned down by General Dyer without any warning. 379 died and 1200 were injured according to official estimates while unofficial estimates put the number of dead and wounded each at a much higher figure. Dyer's only regrets before the Hunter Commission later appointed by the Raj were that his ammunitions ran out and he could not bring his armoured car through the narrow lanes leading to the enclosure. In the weeks following Jallianwallabag, Dyer enforced the martial law in the town with indiscriminate arrests, torture, special tribunals, public flogging, recruitment of lawyers as menials, insistence on "natives" salaaming all "sahibs" and forcing Indians crawl down Kucha Kauchianwala lane where the modesty of a "white" woman had been outraged. Michael 0' Dwyer, the Lt. Governor of the Punjab, treated the country as worse than an enemy territory. He himself conceived the idea of sending aeroplanes to throw bombs upon the rioters and at Gujranwala the crowd was actually machine gunned and bombed from the air. The whole of the Punjab reeled in anguish and pain under a veritable reign of terror, worse than perhaps any that had ever been let loose by any autocracy in Europe.

Extremely grieved at the atrocities committed by the Raj in the Punjab as well as awfully distressed to find that the agitation started by him had not altogether been free from violence, Gandhi admitted his failure to apply *Satyagraha* in its true spirit and regretted his

"Himalayan miscalculation." On 18 April five days after the Jallianwallabag massacre, Gandhi suspended the *Satyagraha* when Ahmedabad was gripped with mob violence. Pandit Madan Mohan Malaviya, Swami Shradhananda and others organised relief work in the Punjab as soon as martial law was withdrawn and a committee was appointed "to conduct an enquiry into the recent occurrences in the Punjab." Malaviya exposed the reign of terror in the Punjab by framing 92 questions alleging specific instances of brutality for the Central Legislative Council which sent such a thrill of horror throughout the length and breadth of the whole country that Chelmsford announced the appointment of a commission of inquiry under Hunter in his opening speech in the Council and immediately introduced and passed an Indemnity Bill protecting the civil and the military officials in the Punjab from the consequences of their action. The unprecedented scale of British repression prevented most Indian politicians from organising a public protest meeting and it was left to Rabindranath Tagore to express the anger and agony of the nation by relinquishing his knighthood in a dignified letter to the Viceroy, on 30 May 1919, "giving voice to the protest of the millions of our countrymen surprised into a dumb anguish of terror."

In the meantime the Government of India Act of 1919 based on the reform proposals of Montagu and Chelmsford had been passed by the British Parliament. The Act set up a Council of State and a Legislative Assembly, with elected majorities but no control over ministers at the Centre and introduced dyarchy in the Provinces where departments with less political weight and little funds like education, health, agriculture and local bodies were transferred to ministers responsible to the Provincial Legislatures. Officials were given control of more vital departments like law and order or finance and the Provincial Governors, like the Viceroy at the Centre, were given powers to veto plus "certificate" procedure of pushing through rejected bills. Revenue resources were divided between the Centre and the Provinces and despite some criticisms of the separate electorates made in the report in 1918, the Act of 1919 not only retained communal representation and reservations but extended them by conceding the Justice Party demands for non-Brahmin reservation in Madras.

Within a few days of the passing of the Act, the Congress held its session in December 1919 at Amritsar where Gandhi emerged as the unquestioned leader of the national movement. Motilal Nehru appealed to the Liberals who had boycotted the Delhi Congress last year to come back, responding to the call of "the lacerated heart of the Punjab" but the appeal went unheeded. Gandhi persuaded the Congress which had already denounced the Montagu-Chelmsford reform proposals when published in 1918 as unsatisfactory to soften its attitude to give the Act of 1919 a fair trial. Despite Gandhi's opposition, a compromise clause describing the Act as "inadequate, unsatisfactory and disappointing" was added mainly at the instance of Tilak, C.R. Das, Rambhuj Dutt Chaudhuri and Hasrat Mohani.

When the new year opened, the political tension generated by "the Reforms Act", the Rowlatt Act and the British repression till December 1919, was further aggravated by the Khilafat question which now occupied the attention of the Congress.

Chapter 22

Khilafat and Non-Co-operation

With the defeat of Turkey and the spread of rumours about very harsh terms being prepared by the victorious Allies, the Khilafat question—the question about the future of the Turkish Sultan—Khalifa——was causing increasing concern among the Indian Muslims since 1919. In March 1920 Muhammad Ali presented three central demands to the diplomats in Paris to leave (a) the Turkish Sultan—Khalifa—with the control over the Muslim sacred places and (b) with sufficient territory to enable him to defend the Islamic faith and finally (c) to allow Arabia, Syria, Iraq, and Palestine to remain under the Muslim sovereignty. Muhammed Ali as well as his brother Shaukat Ali represented the radical section of the Khilafat Movement, consisting of journalists and ulema with considerable influence over small towns and villages, particularly in the United Provinces, Bengal, Sind and Malabar. It was this group which gave a call for hartal on 17 October 1919 and a call for Non-Co-operation at the Delhi All-India Khilafat Conference on 22-23 November 1919 which had elected Gandhi as its President.

Gandhi made himself vital to this group led by the Ali brothers as well as to the Moderate group consisting of prosperous Bombay merchants who organised the Central Khilafat Committee. In the beginning Gandhi supported the Bombay group but with the publication of the very harsh terms of the Treaty of Sevres with

Turkey on 14 May 1920, followed after fourteen days, of the Hunter Commission Report on the Punjab disturbances, Gandhi's stand changed. Gandhi described the *Report* as "page after page of thinly disguised official whitewash." The British Raj had already protected its Punjab officials by an Indemnity Act—now Michael 0' Dwyer was acquitted of blame. On the top of this, in England the House of Lords rejected the censure motion passed on Dyer by the House of Commons, and an English daily, the *Morning Post* raised by subscriptions a purse of £ 26,000 for the butcher of Jallianwallabagh.

Backed by Gandhi, the Allahabad meeting of the Central Khilafat Committee attended by a number of nationalist Hindu leaders, in the first week of June 1920, saw the victory of the radicals. Boycott of titles, civil services, police and army was announced and the movement was started on 1 August 1920, a day also memorable for the death of Tilak. Gandhi saw in the Khilafat Movement an opportunity for cementing Hindu-Muslim unity as "will not occur for another hundred years." Gandhi now pressed the Congress to adopt a similar plan of campaign around the three issues of the Punjab wrong, the Khilafat wrong and the *Swaraj* which was left deliberately undefined. While Gujarat and Bihar initially provided the full support, C.R Das and the Tilakites bitterly opposed the plan. Motilal Nehru, unlike his son, Jawaharlal, was at first hesitant about the crucial issue of boycott of Council elections scheduled for November 1920 but his hesitancy disappeared when he read the summaries of the Hunter Commission Report and wrote to his son on 27 June 1920: "My blood is boiling ever since I read the summaries you have sent. We must hold a special Congress now and raise a veritable hell for the rascals." At the special Congress at Calcutta, summoned in the first week of September 1920, Motilal Nehru's support now proved decisive. And a programme involving surrender of titles, boycott of schools, courts and Councils and of British goods as well as encouragement of national schools, arbitration courts and Khadi was approved.

The December 1920 session of the Nagpur Congress saw the dramatic switch-over of C.R. Das to the support of the plan adopted earlier at the Calcutta special Congress. And the whole Congress whose creed was now modified to "the attainment of Swaraj by all legitimate and peaceful means" lay at Gandhi's feet. Gandhi now utilised his powerful position in revolutionising the structure of the Congress organisation by giving it a new constitution. A small 15 member Working Committee which was to be the real executive head, an All-India Committee of 350 and Provincial Committees with roots going down to districts, towns, talukas and villages were created. The Working Committee was to be a homogeneous body, the All-India Congress Committee was to discuss important matters including a review of the Working Committee decisions and the Provincial Committees were to be reorganised on a linguistic basis, with the number of delegates to the annual session of the Congress to be fixed in proportion to population. An annual subscription of only four annas was to bring the Congress within the reach of India's poor millions which became more youthful when the age limit for membership was reduced to 18. After having thus strengthened the Congress as a political party which also started a Tilak Swaraj Fund to make its position financially secure, Gandhi was now ready to provide leadership in the campaign against the "satanic government," co-operation with which "in any shape or form" he declared to be "sinful."

The Non-Co-operation Movement began with massive student strikes at Calcutta and Lahore. C.R. Das and Motilal Nehru gave up their lucrative legal practice and Subhas Chandra Bose resigned from the Covenanted Civil Service. In April 1921 the Vijayawada session of the All-India Congress Committee decided to concentrate on raising rupees one crore over Tilak Swaraj Fund, enrolling one crore Congress members by throwing the gates of the Congress open to any one accepting its goal and principles as well as by reducing the age-limit for membership to eighteen and installing 20 lakh charkhas for spinning by 30 June. As the country was "not yet sufficiently disciplined, organised and ripe," decision of civil disobedience was postponed. Yet in the face of mounting pressures from new members, the Bombay All-India Congress Committee meeting of 28-30 July permitted boycott of foreign cloth and its public bonfires as well as of the forthcoming visit of the Prince of Wales in November, though full-scale civil disobedience through non-payment of taxes was postponed again. While in the Punjab, poor Sikh peasants revolted against gross evils and abuses prevailing in some Sikh temples, in Malabar, the Muslim peasants known as Moplahs, rose against money-lenders and landlords who were mostly Hindus. It was at the Bombay All-India Congress Committee meeting that Gandhi had given a call for "jail bharo"— "our triumph consists in thousands being led to prisons like lambs to the slaughter house." About its impact, Nehru gives us a very amusing story that the superintendent of the packed Lucknow prison used to tell the jailor, who was a Khan Sahib, that if he could succeed in allowing some of the Congress prisoners to escape, then he would be recommended for the title of Khan Bahadur. On 17 November the Prince of Wales was greeted with an extremely successful hartal all over India. However, there were violent clashes in Bombay, which made Gandhi declare: "Swaraj has stuck in my nostrils." He once again postponed his plans for starting civil disobedience in the selected taluka of Bardoli.

The policy of the British Raj now headed by Chelmsford's successor, Reading, of mass arrests including wives and children of political leaders and ban on press, public meetings and volunteer groups raised by the Congress for the "jail bharo" programme threatened, to alienate the Liberals. While angered by the jailing of the Ali brothers in November for speeches at the Karachi Khilafat Conference in July, Hasrat Mohani and other Khilafat leaders were demanding complete independence and giving up of the non-violence dogma at the December Ahmedabad Congress. The Ahmedabad Congress was presided over by Hakim Ajmal Khan in the absence of C.R.Das, the President-elect of the session, in jail. The Congress advised its workers to organise individual civil disobedience and mass civil disobedience only when the mass of people had been sufficiently trained in the methods of non-violence. Gandhi was appointed "the sole executive authority of the Congress with the power, to appoint a successor in emergency."

Gandhi addressed a conference of local people at Bardoli in Gujarat on 30 January 1922. At Bardoli the 4000 Khaddar-clad representatives and 500 women adopted a resolution to begin a mass civil disobedience under the guidance of Gandhi and Vallabhbhai Patel. Gandhi finally conveyed his decision to Reading on 1 February to start the civil disobedience which was to take the form of a no-revenue campaign at Bardoli on the issue of infringed freedom of speech, press and association. The civil disobedience was to begin from the second week of February. However, when the news of the burning alive of 22 policemen by angry but provoked peasants at Chauri Chaura, Gorkhpur on 5 February, reached Gandhi, he called off his mass civil disobedience at Bardoli as well as the entire Non-Co-operation Movement on 11 February with the approval of the Congress Working Committee meeting at Bardoli on 11 and 12 February. On 16 February, 1922 he wrote in *Young India*: "I would suffer every humiliation, every torture, absolute ostracism and death itself to prevent the movement from becoming violent."

When the All-India Congress Committee met at Delhi, a few days later, on 24 and 25 February, to consider the question of suspension, there was a strong opposition. Many among its members considered Gandhi's action not only a great blunder but a severe blow to the national movement. As a matter of fact, events in the last two months of 1921 had almost been moving towards a Congress victory when Reading, in secret telegrams to Montagu in December 1921, had suggested not only release of prisoners, but a Round Table Conference and an early revision of the just-implemented Reform Scheme—a suggestion, certainly an interesting anticipation of the 1930s, which was scotched partly by Gandhi's refusal of any compromise and partly by a reluctant

British Cabinet to show any leniency at this stage. At the All-India Congress Committee meeting in Delhi, Gandhi tried hard to maintain that the resolution of suspension did not in any way nullify the December 1920 Nagpur Congress resolution of Non-Co-operation. Yet as the Congress Enquiry Committee revealed later in 1922 that "there can be no doubt that the principle and policy laid down at Abmedabad were completely reversed to the great disappointment of an expectant public" and the Congress "failed to create sufficient enthusiasm to carry on the constructive programme [of spinning, weaving and untouchability] with the earnestness it deserved." Indeed there was great disappointment among Gandhi's followers in the Congress and as Jawaharlal Nehru wrote: "We were angry when we learned of this stoppage of our struggle at a time when we seemed to be consolidating our position and advancing on all fronts. The sudden suspension of our movement after the Chauri Chaura incident was resented, I think, by almost all the Congress leaders—other than Gandhi, of course. My father (who was in jail at the time) was much upset by it. The young people were even more agitated. Our mounting hopes tumbled to the ground and this mental reaction was to be expected."

The British Raj which had not dared touch Gandhi before Chauri Chaura now exploited the feeling of repulsion against Gandhi among his followers. Gandhi was arrested on 10 March 1922 and tried on 18 March at Ahmedabad. He was sentenced to six years' simple imprisonment. The news did not produce any expected upheaval in any part of the country.

Whatever may be the contemporary reactions to Gandhi's cry for a halt after Chauri Chaura, it cannot be denied that the ultimate gain of the movement outweighed its immediate losses. With an increasing recognition of social evils like untouchability and drinking and of Khadi as an answer to rural needs, the unsophisticated villagers became alive of their economic problems and their political cause and began to talk of "Gandhi Swaraj" as a remedy for their ills including payment of high taxes. It was Gandhi who "converted the nationalist movement into a revolutionary movement" and restructured the loose Congress organisation after the December 1920 Nagpur Congress into a solid and strong, secular and popular political party in India to fight the British Raj. The apparent failure of the movement did not bother him much at the moment as he himself explained: "The fight that was commenced in 1920 is a fight to finish, whether it lasts one month or one year or many months or many years."

Chapter 23

Swarajya Party

The arrest and imprisonment of Gandhi in March 1922 was followed by the appointment of a Civil Disobedience Enquiry Committee by the All-India Congress Committee which met at Lucknow in the first week of June 1922. The Enquiry Committee chaired by Hakim Ajmal Khan consisted of Motilal Nehru, C. Rajagopalachri, M.A. Ansari, Vithalbhai Patel and Kasturiranga Iyengar as members. In October 1922 the Committee submitted its report which revealed a division among its members. While Ansari, Rajagopalachari and Iyengar wanted to concentrate on Gandhian constructive work like spinning, weaving and untouchables, Motilal Nehru, Vithalbhai Patel and Ajmal Khan argued for Congress participation in Council elections following a changed situation in the country. Both groups—the Pro-Changers and No-Changers—put its views separately in the form of minutes which formed nearly two fifths of the entire report. The subject was referred by All-India Congress Committee which met at Calcutta in November to the forthcoming Congress session at Gaya in December 1922 for a decision. The Committee at its Calcutta meeting advised the Provincial Congress Committee to sanction limited civil disobedience as the country was not prepared for mass civil disobedience.

C.R. Das, the President of the Congress session at Gaya in December 1922 argued vigorously in his presidential address on behalf of the Pro-Changers and suggested that the Congress should enter the Councils to wreck the reforms from within by "uniform,

"uniform, consistent and continuous obstruction" of their proceedings. "The only successful boycott of these Councils," he said, "is either to mend them in a manner suitable to the attainment of Swaraj or to end them completely." It seemed Das as President would carry the day but the case of the No-Changers was successfully argued by the orthodox Gandhians including Rajendra Prasad and Vallabhbhai Patel and the Congress decided in favour of the No-Changers by rejecting Council entry.

However, C.R. Das and Motilal Nehru went ahead and in March 1923 they set up a Swarajya Party to contest the forthcoming Council elections in November to wreck reforms, from within. The All-India Congress Committee meeting in Bombay in May 1923 resolved that no propaganda be carried on amongst voters relating to the boycott of Councils to counter the canvassing of the Swarajyists. The danger of a formal split in the Congress was, however, averted by the special Congress in Delhi on 15 September 1923, which struck a compromise by allowing the Congressmen to stand for Council elections while emphasising the need for concentrating on "the constructive programme of Gandhi" for the attainment of Swaraj "at the earliest possible moment by united endeavour."

In the November 1923 elections the Swarajyists won a majority in the Central Provinces where the Tilakites like N.C. Kelkar had never been particularly enamoured of the Non-Co-operation Movement and in Bengal where young B.C. Roy defeated the old stalwart Surendra Nath Banerjea who as a Liberal had become a minister in 1921. The Swarajyists' programme of wrecking the reforms from within started with their refusal of salaries to dyarchy ministers in the Central Provinces and Bengal, compelling them to repeatedly use their "certificate" powers to push through legislation. The Swarajyists thus proved dyarchy to be no real constitutional advance. In the Central Legislative Assembly where the Swarajyists had formed a coalition with the Liberals and Muslim League members, a resolution demanding a Round Table Conference to discuss reforms leading to responsible government was passed at the initiative of the Swarajyists in February 1924.

In the meantime the No-Changers had not been quite convinced about the correctness of the Swarajyists' stand. Their hopes were revived when in February 1924 Gandhi was released from jail, on the ground of ill-health. At the All-India Congress Committee session at Ahmedabad in June 1924 Gandhi moved a resolution prescribing a minimum spinning qualification for the Congress membership and another removing those who had entered Councils from the ranks of the Congress office bearers. Both the resolutions were defeated. At the November 1924 Belgaum Congress which was presided over by Gandhi, a compromise was struck between the Swarajyists and Gandhi. The Swarajyists agreed to Gandhi's constructive programme including introduction of a spinning qualification for the Congress membership and Gandhi, on the other hand, agreed to their work in the Councils "as an integral part of the Congress organization."

In 1925 Gandhi decided to place the entire organisational machinery of the Congress at the disposal of the Swarajyists and devoted his whole energy to the constructive programme. Besides spinning he directed his attention to the promotion of Hindu—Muslim unity and the uplift of the untouchables, described by him as Harijans. His sincere effort and personal example removed the thousand year-old inertia of the Hindu society and a genuine movement to improve the condition of the Harijans stirred the whole country. He thus severely kept himself away from any active political work and his announcement that 1926 would be a "year of silence" for him led many to believe that Gandhi was quitting active politics.

By 1926 also the politics of Council entry was leading to a host of problems including internal dissensions. Some of the Swarajyists including Madan Mohan Malaviya, Lala Lajpat Rai and N.C. Kelkar had formed themselves into a group of "Responsivists" and had offered co-operation to the British Raj, with acceptance of executive posts. C.R. Das also seemed to have toyed with the idea of responsive co-operation in his Faridpur Conference speech of May 1925 just before his sudden death in

June 1925. In Bengal the death of C.R. Das was followed by a bitter succession war for leadership between J.M. Sengupta and Birendranath Sasmal. And in the Central Legislative Assembly the Swarajyists having failed to achieve much despite their work in co-operation with the Moderates and the Muslim League members, decided to walk out in March 1926.

On the eve of the 1926 elections, Madan Mohan Malaviya, Motilal's old rival, formed an Independent Congress Party in alliance with the Responsive Co-operators like Lajpat Rai. The programme of the Party reflected an uninhibited Hindu communalism possibly as an answer to the communal passions that had been sweeping the country since the suspension of the Non-Co-operation Movement in February 1922. With the suspension of the movement, the glowing prospect of a Hindu-Muslim entente, as visualised by Gandhi, had "dissolved like a summer thundercloud." In September 1924 a 21-day fast by Gandhi at the house of Muhammad Ali Khan led to Hindu-Muslim unity conference but restoration of harmony could not be achieved. The alliance between the Congress and the Khilafat leaders lingered on till early 1925 when Muhammed Ali broke with Gandhi in the wake of repeated riots. With the transformation of Turkey into a modern secular state and abolition of the Turkish Caliphate in 1924 by Kamal Attaturk there was no programme now for a joint Hindu-Muslim action. The Muslim League, now reinforced by the Khilafat leaders who no longer took their inspiration from Gandhi grew stronger and revived the old ideas of Syed Ahmad Khan. It was the communal discord which proved to be the undoing of the Swarajya Party which went down everywhere in the 1926 elections except in Madras before the combination of Hindu Mahasabha and Responsive Co-operators. The British Raj's policy towards the Congress demand for self-government remained unchanged and the niggardly policy of granting too little concessions, and that too not until it was too late, sustained the struggle for freedom. At the moment however, the freedom movement seemed to have struck a very bad patch.

Chapter 24

Simon Commission

The drooping spirit of the national movement was soon replaced by a vigorous enthusiasm for action by an announcement of the British Government of a commission on 8 November 1927 to enquire into, and report on, the working of the reforms as a basis for further action. As per the provision of the Act of 1919, the first such enquiry was to be held after ten years in 1929 when British elections would be held. Since there was a growing probability that the Labour Party would return to power, it was considered safer to forestall the Labour Government by advancing the date by two years. The Commission was to consist of seven British Members of Parliament including Attlee under Sir John Simon.

The exclusion of Indians from a body which was to prepare the future constitution of India was so unnatural that the announcement was received with profound disappointment and righteous indignation by all political leaders, irrespective of their party affiliations, and they unanimously decided to boycott the Commission. "The reasons for the boycott," declared Ansari, the Congress President at the Madras session of 1927, "are of the most cogent description. Indian people are entitled to determine their own Constitution either by a Round Table Conference or by a Convention Parliament. That claim has been definitely negatived by the appointment of the Commission. That is the most important reason not only from the Congress point of view but from the point of view of all the Indian political parties which concurred in the two resolutions of the Legislative Assembly of 18th February, 1924, and 8th September 1925. That of course is the fundamental objection. The second reason is that we cannot be parties to an enquiry into our fitness for Swaraj or for any measure of responsible government. Our claim for Swaraj is there and it is only a question of negotiations and settlement between the British Government and the Indian people. The third reason is undoubtedly the affront to Indian self-respect involved in the deliberate exclusion of Indians from the Commission."

While the proposal of boycotting the Simon Commission was accepted by all political parties, the Congress suggested some practical measures to make it more effective. These were: first, mass demonstration all over India on the day the members of the Commission arrived in India and similar demonstrations in every city on the day it was visited by them; second, refusal of legislatures to help or elect their own committees to co-operate with the Commission and rejection of the demand for grant of money in connection with the work of the Commission; and finally social boycott of the members of the Commission.

On 3 February 1928, the day of the arrival of the Commission in Bombay, complete hartal was observed in all important towns in India and huge demonstrations marched in processions waving black flags and carrying banners: "Go back, Simon." In Bombay on that day nearly fifty thousand people assembled in the Chaupatti beach to strongly condemn in one voice the action of the British Government. As the Commission toured the country in 1928, city after city was rocked by the shouts of "Go back, Simon." The massive demonstrations in Calcutta on 13 February when the Commission visited that city was followed on 1 March by a call for boycott of British goods. In Lahore on 30 October Lajpat Rai was wounded in a wanton police assault from which he never recovered and died on 17 November. In Lucknow on 28-30 November Khaliquzzaman floated kites and balloons with "Go back, Simon" slogans over a talukdar's reception to the Commission at Kaiserbagh. Govinda Ballabh Pant received serious injuries from a police lathi charge in the anti-Simon demonstrations at Lucknow from which he never fully recovered and Jawaharlal Nehru was another victim of this humiliating treatment. The whole of India was thus once again in ferment and an intended gesture of the British Government became a rallying cry for freedom.

A more positive aspect of the appointment of Simon Commission was the formulation of a scheme of Indian constitution acceptable to all parties. Lord Birkenhead, the Secretary of State. challenged the Swarajyist Party "to produce a constitution which carries behind it a fair measure of general agreement among the great peoples of India" while announcing the appointment of Simon Commission. The question was taken up by the Congress at its Madras session in December 1927. The Congress authorised the Working Committee to get in touch with similar Committees of other organisations to draft a constitution for India and to place it before a special convention of all parties in Delhi, not later than March 1928. The December 1927 session of the Muslim League offered a compromise formula which was accepted by the Congress joint electorates in place of separate electorates with reserved seats for minorities, a promise of one -third Muslim representation in the Central Assembly, representation in proportion to population in the Punjab and Bengal and the three new Muslim-majority provinces of Sind, Baluchistan and North-West Frontier provinces—though the breakaway League session at Lahore under Mohommed Shafi refused to give up separate electorates and decided to co-operate with the Simon Commission. Thus all established political groups except the Justice Party in Madras and the Punjab Unionists began preparing for an All Parties Conference to draw up a constitution.

The All Parties Conference held its first meeting at Delhi on 12 February 1928 under M.A. Ansari and appointed a committee under Motilal Nehru to draft the constitution and at its third meeting in Lucknow in August 1928 accepted the report on the constitution drafted mainly by Motilal Nehru and the Liberal Party leader, Tej Bahadur Sapru. The report, also known as the Nehru Report, made a number of concessions to the Hindu Mahasabha which at its Jabbalpur session under N.C. Kelkar in April 1928 had bitterly opposed the creation of new Muslim-majority provinces and reservation of seats for majorities in the Punjab and Bengal which would ensure Muslim control over legislatures in both. While there would be joint electorates everywhere, reserved seats were conceded only at the Centre and in provinces with Muslims minorities and not in the Punjab and Bengal. Sind would be detached from Bombay and made into a separate province only after India acquired Dominion Status and subject to a weightage for the Hindu minority there, with a broadly unitary political structure in which the Centre would keep the residual powers. Jinnah who had broken with the Shafi-Fazl-i-Husain group of the Punjab Muslims on the joint electorates and who could legitimately accuse the Congress leaders of going back on their December 1927 promises made a desperate attempt at unity at the last session of All Parties Conference in Calcutta in December 1928 but his attempt was frustrated by the Hindu Mahasabha leader, M.R. Jayakar. Jinnah now rejoined the Shafi group and in March 1929 put forward his famous "Fourteen Points" which repeated the demands for new provinces, one-third seats at the Centre, and federation with complete provincial autonomy, and revived the slogan of separate electorates—till such a time as the other points were accepted by the Hindus.

The Nehru Report which thus attempted to solve the problem of communal representation was also remarkable in other aspects as the first Indian attempt to draft a constitutional framework for the country, providing for responsible government both in the Centre and the provinces, complete with lists of central and provincial subjects and fundamental rights. It was very natural for a moderate body like the All Parties Conference to advocate

Dominion Status, and not complete independence which was declared as the goal by the Madras Congress in December 1927 and later discussed and approved by the Provincial Conferences in the Punjab, Delhi and the United Provinces. The younger section of the Congress led by Jawaharlal Nehru and Subhas Chandra Bose, who together had set up the Independence League to popularise the idea of complete independence was very unhappy with this modification of the Congress goal. Gandhi, by way of a compromise, suggested after lively discussions in the Congress session at Calcutta in December 1928 under Motilal Nehru that the Dominion Status be accepted provided the British Parliament accepted the Nehru Constitution in its entirety within a year from then, that is, by 31 December 1929. If not, the Congress would revert to its Madras goal of complete independence or *Purna Swaraj* and would organise a campaign of non-violent Non-Co-operation.

Chapter 25

Civil Disobedience and Round Table

In June 1929 the Labour Party came to power in Britain. At the suggestion of Simon, the Prime Minister Ramsay MacDonald, extended the terms of reference of the Simon Commission to examine future relationship between British India and the Indian States and decided on a conference between their representatives and the British Government after the publication of the Commission's report to obtain the greatest possible measure of agreement. MacDonald invited Irwin who had succeeded Reading as the Viceroy to London for consultation and on his return to Delhi, issued a statement on 31 October 1929, in which he stated "the natural issue of India's constitutional progress" was to be "the attainment of Dominion Status." An All Parties Conference at Delhi in November offered to co-operate with Irwin in evolving a Dominion Constitution for India on these conditions that the proposed Round Table Conference should discuss the details, and not the basic principles, of Dominion Status; second, the Congress should have a majority representation in the Conference and finally a general amnesty should be declared before the Conference met. Subhas Chandra Bose refused to sign the Delhi statement and Jawaharalal Nehru who did, soon developed strong doubts. However, when Gandhi, Jinnah and others met Irwin on 23 December, he pointed out "that he was unable to prejudge or commit the Conference at all to any particular line," following strong

Tory attack on his 31 October Delhi statement in the British Parliament. Negotiations broke down as no guarantee of immediate Dominion Status was forthcoming and Gandhi now declared himself definitely for complete independence or *Purna Swaraj*. "I have burnt my boat," he said.

It was in this circumstance that after a few days on 28 December the Lahore Congress met under Jawaharlal Nehru who had described himself in 1928 as "a truant and errant child" of Gandhi in politics. Nehru was nominated as President of the Lahore Congress by Gandhi as a recognition of the rising youth power within the Congress. As Gandhi wrote in *Young India* in September 1929: "Steam becomes a mighty power only when it allows itself to be imprisoned. Even so have the youth of the country of their own free will to allow their inexhaustible energy to be imprisoned, controlled and set free in strictly measured and required quantities." He wanted to use the youth as a mighty power through Jawaharlal Nehru who was "undoubtedly an extremist, thinking far ahead of his surroundings" but "humble and practical enough not to force to the breaking point."

Gandhi's description of Jawaharlal Nehru as "an extremist" in September 1929 represented a mental development that came to Nehru when he was invited to participate in the Brussels Congress against Colonial Oppression and Imperialism in February 1927. His active participation in the Brussels Congress gave him a vision of anti-imperialist solidarity of socialist and nationalist forces in Asia and Africa which he never totally abandoned. He was appointed a Honorary President of the League against Imperialism and for National Independence organised at Brussels. In November 1927, Jawaharlal Nehru along with his father Motilal, went to visit the Soviet Union, on invitation and the articles that he wrote for the *Hindu* covering this visit vividly reflect the deep impact made on him by the "country of the hammer and sickle, where workers and peasants sit on the thrones of the mighty."

In his stirring presidential address, Nehru put the freedom movement in India in an international perspective with radical overtones. "I must frankly confess that I am a socialist and a republican," Nehru declared, "and am no believer in kings and princes or in the order which produces the modern kings of industry." The Lahore Congress declared that the word "Swaraj" in Article 1 of the Congress Constitution should mean complete independence and further declared the entire scheme of the Nehru Committee's report to have lapsed, and hoped that all Congressmen would henceforth devote their exclusive attention to the attainment of complete independence for India. The All-India Congress Committee was authorised to launch upon a programme of civil disobedience after rejecting Subhas Chandra Bose's alternative proposal for immediate non-payment of taxes, general strikes wherever and whenever possible and "a parallel government." The Lahore Congress set a seal upon the future destiny of India when on 31 December, as the clock struck midnight, and the date of ultimatum issued by the last Congress session at Calcutta expired, Nehru came out in a solemn procession to the banks of the Ravi and hoisted the tri-colour flag of Indian independence in the presence of a mammoth gathering braving the biting cold of Lahore winter, amidst shouts, not merely just of *Bande Mataram*, but *Inquilab Zindabad*. The Lahore Congress of 1929 thus made "a tryst with destiny."

The Congress Working Committee which was reorganised by Gandhi excluding Bose and Srinivasa Iyengar met on 2 January 1930 and implemented the Congress resolution of the boycott of the Councils. The Committee decided that 26 January 1930 should be observed all over India as the *Purna Swaraj* day and a manifesto, drafted by Gandhi and adopted by the Committee, denouncing the British Raj for having "ruined India economically, politically, culturally and spiritually," asserting that it was "a crime against man and God" to submit any longer to such a rule, and calling for preparations for "civil disobedience, including non-

-payment of taxes," was to be read on that occasion to the people in the villages and towns and assent of the audience was to be taken by a show of hands. In an article in *Young India* on 31 January Gandhi offered to Irwin an 11 point ultimatum listing specific national grievances for redressal, which seemed to many a sad climb down from the *Purna Swaraj* resolution, since no demand was made for any change in the political structure not even Dominion Status.

The Working Committee met again in mid-February on the banks of the Sabarmati to authorise Gandhi and his followers firmly believing in non-violence to start civil disobedience but Gandhi kept the whole country in an animated suspense. When asked by Rabindranath Tagore about his plan of action, Gandhi replied: "I am thinking furiously, day and night, and I do not see any light coming out of the darkness." Gandhi's hesitancy may be explained partly by the fact that he knew that he was to lead an unarmed people against an armed power who would win if violence were let loose and partly by his assurance to his fellow Congressmen "that civil disobedience when it came, will not be stopped because of a sporadic act of violence." At last on 2 March 1930 he communicated his decision to launch *Satyagraha* at Dandi, a village on the sea-coast, about 200 miles from Sabarmati, where he would manufacture salt by violating the salt law. On 5 March he wrote to Irwin asking for immediate removal of the grievances in the "eleven points," failing which he would start civil disobedience. Jawaharlal Nehru was compelled to remark: "What was the point of making a list of our political and social reforms when we were talking in terms of Independence? Did Gandhiji mean the same thing when he used this term as we did, or did we speak a different language?" Nehru also recalled in his *Autobiography* his initial sense of bewilderment over the choice of salt as the central issue. As expected Irwin refused to see Gandhi and regretted that Gandhi's action was clearly bound to "involve violation of law and danger to the public peace."

Gandhi began his Dandi March with a chosen band of 79 male and female members on 12 March 1930. As he walked, leaning on his stick, villagers flocked to see Gandhi on his way to break a law which by taxes, increased the price of a daily necessity. Village officials resigned their posts and volunteers poured into his ranks to join what became a non-violent column marching on Dandi. And on 6 April when Gandhi violated the salt law by manufacturing salt at Dandi, the nation received its signal and country-wide violation of salt law began. Gandhi's slow march over 241 miles in 24 days with full publicity to the world through Indian and foreign newspapers correspondents who followed him from Sabarmati to Dandi made a profound impact on all and roused the masses to the coming struggle for *Swaraj* as contemplated by the Congress. On 10 April Gandhi made a special appeal in *Young India* to the women to take the work of picketing and spinning and there was an immediate response when thousands of women came out of their seclusion to offer civil disobedience. Formerly only women from the families of national leaders like C.R. Das and Motilal Nehru or colleges in the large cities had taken part in public political demonstrations. Now far more women joined the movement as could be seen from the fact that in a socially conservative city like Delhi in those days, 1600 women were imprisoned for political activity. The Home Secretary confessed to Verrier Elwin, a former Oxford Don, that nothing had disturbed him more than the great awakening among Indian women and the part they had begun to play in politics. The presence of women in their midst redoubled the energy and activities of the men and spurred them on to the greater efforts and sacrifices for the country. After violating the salt law at Dandi, Gandhi announced his intention of raiding the salt depot at Dharsana in Surat. He was arrested and put into prison before he could set out for Dharsana and his place was taken by Abbas Tyabji who was also arrested. Sarojini Naidu hurried to Dharsana and nearly with 2500 volunteers from all parts of Gujarat raided the salt depot on 21 May. Webb Miller, an

American journalist who was a witness to Naidu's Dharsana raid and left a vivid description of it in a book later published, commented: "At times, the spectacle of unresisting men being methodically bashed into bloody pulps sickened me so much that I had to turn away. I felt an indefinable sense of helpless rage and loathing."

Gandhi's arrest, in mid-May was followed by organised demonstrations throughout India. The Working Committee now sanctioned, besides boycott of British goods, cloth and liquor which had accompanied violation of salt law everywhere, non-payment of revenue in the ryotwari provinces and a no chaukidari tax campaign in Zamindari provinces and violation of forest laws in the Central Provinces. The movement spread to the North West Frontier Province where the red-shirt volunteers of Abdul Ghaffar Khan, better know as Frontier Gandhi, followed in a non- violent manner, an intense anti-government movement in various ways including non-payment of taxes. Barring this as well as few isolated pockets like Delhi, Muslim participation remained at a low key level following the breakdown of the Nehru Report negotiations and a decade of intensive communalism and fratricidal strife. Yet the movement rose, as had been observed by Verrier Elwin, to a pitch of sincerity and devotion that had rarely been equalled in the political upheavals of the world.

At first the British Raj looked upon Gandhi's decision to violate salt laws at Dandi with ridicule and contempt. Irwin complacently informed the Secretary of State, Wedgewood-Benn that the prospect of a salt campaign did not "keep me awake at night" and an English daily (*The Statesman*) taunted: "The Mahatma could go on boiling sea-water till Dominion Status was attained." Yet before long the movement reached such a dimension that it upset the Raj's anticipation. And the Raj took recourse to repression through mass arrests, lathi-charge, torture and firing. The Congress Working Committee meeting on 21 January 1931 described some of the aspects of the British repressive policy as "the imprisonment of about 75 thousand innocent men and women, numerous indiscriminate and brutal lathi-charges, various forms of torture even of those in custody, firing resulting in the maiming and deaths of hundred of people, looting of property, burning of houses and marching of moving columns of armed police and *Sawars* and British soldiers in several rural parts, depriving people of the right of public speech, and association by prohibiting meetings and processions and declaring Congress and allied associations unlawful, forfeiting their movables and occupying their houses and offices."

While the whole of India was thus convulsed by the Civil Disobedience Movement, the Simon Commission published its report on 7 June 1930. It recommended: (1) Federal Constitution for India; (2) Full Provincial autonomy subject to some overiding powers vested in the Governor: (3) Enlargement of the Provincial Legislative Councils as well as of the Lower House of the Central Legislature and (4) Separation of Burma from India. Irwin privately admitted to Wedgewood-Benn on 19 June that the *Report* "will provoke an explosion here" by its "stern refusal anywhere to mention Dominion Status." The recommendations were fully rejected by the Indian Legislative Assembly though without any Congress member then and the National Liberal Federation demanded that these must not form the basis of the forthcoming Round Table Conference. The Congress leaders, then in jail, were allowed to confer. Gandhi and Nehru issued a joint statement from Yeravda jail in Poona on 15 August 1930 asserting that the Congress would not accept any solution which did not guarantee, first, India's right to secede from the British Empire; second, a national government responsible to the people including control of defence and finance and finally India's right to submit to an impartial tribunal all British claims and concessions given to the Britishers in the past.

The British Government did not pay any heed to the protest of the Congress and in accordance with the declaration of Irwin on

31 October 1929, summoned the First Round Table Conference at London on 12 November 1930 which was inaugurated by the King. The Conference continued till 19 January 1931, which was presided over by the British Prime Minister, Ramsay MacDonald and attended by 89 members,—16 from the British Political Parties, 16 from the Indian states, and 57 from British India. The Congress did not participate in the Conference though representatives of other political parties and minority groups—the National Liberal Federation, the Muslim League, the Depressed Classes, the Sikhs—did attend it. There was a general agreement among the Indian members that the British India and the Indian States should form a Federal Union ruled by a Parliamentary System of government. The British members, however, opposed the immediate grant of Dominion Status and the introduction of British Parliamentary system in India. There were prolonged discussions on the framework of the federation leading to an agreement on Dominion Status though the minority problem remained unsolved. B.R. Ambedkar demanded that for electoral purposes the Depressed Classes should be treated as a separate community and the Muslim delegation formally declared that no advance was possible or practicable, whether in the province or in the Centre, without "adequate safeguards" for the Muslims of India and that no constitution would be acceptable to the Muslims of India without such safeguards. In his closing address to the Conference on 19 January 1931 MacDonald declared that "His Majesty's Government will be prepared to recognize the principle of the responsibility of the Executive to the Legislature" since it was realised that a federal assembly with a major section nominated by princes should prove a safe enough body and carefully hedged in the promise of central responsibility with a series of "reservations and safeguards" in the crucial spheres of defence, external affairs and financial control.

One redeeming feature of MacDonald's valedictory address was the hope expressed by him that "those engaged at present in Civil disobedience might respond to the Viceroy's appeal and take their part in the co-operative work that lay ahead." The Congress reacted to it quickly by summoning its Working Committee meeting at Ahmedabad on 21 January, which repudiated the representative character of the Conference and asserted that civil disobedience could not be suspended till most of the members of the Committee and thousands of men and women locked in jail were set free. The Raj responded quickly by releasing the members of the Working Committee on 26 January to afford them an opportunity to discuss the political situation. On 6 February the Indian delegates issued a manifesto after their return which described the Conference as a significant gain for India. The Indian Liberal delegates including Sapru attended the Congress Working Committee meeting at Allahabad on 13 February, which suggested that Gandhi should seek an interview with Irwin who had earlier turned down his demand for an enquiry into the police excesses. Gandhi wrote to the Viceroy on 14 February and the reply granting him the interview came on 16 February. Gandhi left for Delhi on the same day and met Irwin on 17 February.

After protracted negotiations a formal settlement was signed on 5 March 1931. The settlement, known as the Gandhi-Irwin Pact, provided for the release of political prisoners, suspension of the civil disobedience and Congress participation in the Second Round Table Conference. And Gandhi accepted Irwin's insistence on three "Lynch-pins—Federation; Indian responsibility; reservations and safeguards," as outlined at the First Round Table Conference under Clause 2 of the Pact. Gandhi also gave up his demands for enquiry into police atrocities and return of confiscated lands already sold to third parties in return for release of civil disobedience prisoners and token concessions regarding salt and non-political *Swadeshi* propaganda. Gandhi signed the Pact after obtaining the approval of the Working Committee members who had joined him at Delhi.

Clause 2 of the Pact gave Jawaharlal Nehru "a tremendous shock"—"Was it for this that our people had behaved so gallantly for a year? Were all our brave words and deeds to end in this? The independence resolution of the Congress, the pledge of January 26, so often repeated?" Indeed there is no doubt that the Gandhi-Irwin Pact was a far cry from the goal of the Congress as set up at Lahore under Jawarhalal Nehru in December 1929. Gandhi signed the Pact possibly under pressures from the Indian Liberals and other political groups as well as from "a number of Gandhi's followers, particularly among mercantile community" who were "contemplating a breach with him" unless he adopted reasonable attitude as Irwin was informed on 7 February by the Bombay Governor. Purshottamdas Thakurdas who in collaboration with Birla had founded the Federation of Indian Chambers of Commerce and Industry in 1927 went to meet Gandhi at the Working Committee meeting in Allahabad on 13 February "in order to try to put commercial pressure on him" and Thakurdas had been with Gandhi in Delhi during the whole period of his negotiations with the Viceroy.

One important gain for the Congress was an increase of its prestige immediately. The very fact that the Viceroy and Gandhi put their respective signatures together on a document put the Congress on a high pedestal—a fact which was later often resented by Irwin's successor. Gandhi's popularity also increased as could be seen from the fact that immediately after the Pact, on 25 March at Karachi before the Congress session on 29 March, rupees ten thousand were collected from people who came to see and hear Gandhi on an admission fee of four annas per head. It was at this meeting that Gandhi prophesied: "Gandhi may die but Gandhism will live forever."

Nehru who after his father's death on 6 February 1931 had become psychologically dependent on Gandhi spent some sleepless night after the conclusion of the Pact feeling a great emptiness in his heart "as of something precious gone, almost beyond recall." Yet it was he who at the Karachi Congress which met on 29 March under the shadow of the execution of Bhagat Singh and the outbreak of communal violence, moved the key resolution endorsing the Delhi Pact as well as asserting that the Congress delegation at the Conference would work for "the Congress goal of Purna Swaraj." Gandhi who was selected as the Congress delegate at the Conference by the Working Committee meeting on 1 and 2 April was at first reluctant to go in view of the communal riots that had broken out at Karachi as well as of the refusal of Willingdon, despite his predecessor, Irwin's assurances, to nominate the Muslim nationalist Ansari on the ground that the Muslim delegates were opposed to him. Yet at the last moment after a meeting with the Viceroy at Simla Gandhi was persuaded to leave for London by Vallabhbhai Patel and Nehru.

Gandhi arrived at London on 12 September, five days after the start of the Second Round Table Conference which continued till 1 December 1931. Gandhi struck to the Karachi resolution of the Congress, totally oblivious of the decisions already arrived at in the First Round Table Conference and to which he had already subscribed in his agreement with Irwin on 5 March 1931. He demanded immediate establishment of the full responsible government in the Centre as well as in the provinces with complete control over defence, external affairs and finance. Safeguards were not needed and therefore no special powers be given either to the Governors or the Governor-General. However, the session was soon deadlocked on the minorities issue and this time separate electorates were demanded not only by Muslims but by Depressed Castes, Indian Christians, Anglo-Indians, and Europeans and all these groups united in a "minorities pact" for joint action on 13 November. British officials and business representatives like Benthall clamouring for the retention of enormous reserved powers in finance cultivated the Muslim delegates. Gandhi desperately fought against this concerted move to make all constitutional progress conditional on a solution of the communal problem. That solution, he argued, would be "the crown of the Swaraj Constitution and not its foundation" and on 5 October Gandhi even offered to accept all Muslim claims provided they supported the Congress demand for *Swaraj* much to the dislike of Hindu Mahasabha delegates and the Sikhs who were bitterly opposed to any move that could give a majority Muslims in the Punjab. The princes were also speaking in different voices on the federation question and seemed less enthusiastic now than in 1930, as the threat of an immediate change in the Centre had diminished with the calling off its movement by the Congress. A British move to postpone discussion of changes in the Centre altogether could only be scotched by the opposition offered by the otherwise pliable Sapru, Jinnah and Ambedkar. On 1 December MacDonald ended the session with an address which reiterated his 19 January stand, announced the creation of two new Muslim majority provinces, North West Frontier Province and Sind, set up an India Consultative Committee and three expert committees on franchise, finance and states and held out the humiliating and dangerous prospect from the nationalist point of view of a unilateral British Communal Award if the Indians failed to agree.

An out-maneuvered and dejected Gandhi returned home on 28 December only to find Nehru, Tandon and Ghaffar Khan in jail and large scale repressive measures in full swing in Bengal, United Provinces and the North West Frontier Province. Willingdon rudely turned down Gandhi's request for an interview, leaving the Congress Working Committee with no option but to resume civil disobedience. As Jawaharlal Nehru put it about the resumption of civil disobedience including non-payment of taxes: "The initial push of inspiration was far less than in 1930. It was as if we entered unwillingly to battle. There was a glory about it in 1930 which had faded a little two years later."

Smarting under the indignity of Gandhi-Irwin Agreement on 5 March 1931, Willingdon made a deliberate plan not only to force the resumption of civil disobedience upon the Congress but elaborate arrangements and preparations during the period of truce that followed 5 March to grapple with it at a moment's notice. On

4 January 1932 the long-prepared plans for pre-emptive strike went into operation, with a battery of ordinances— Emergency Powers, Unlawful Association, Unlawful Instigation, and Molestation and Boycotting—banning Congress organisations at all levels, arresting leaders, activists and sympathisers, and providing for confiscation of property. No less than 272 associations were banned on the very first day in Bengal alone. There was to be "no drawn battle this time," declared Samuel Hoare, the Conservative Secretary of State for India of the British Government headed by a Labour Prime Minister, Ramsay MacDonald. Out maneuvered and facing repressive measures on an entirely unprecedented scale, the Civil Disobedience Movement under the Congress still fought on valiantly—picketing cloth and liquor shops, markets, pro-raj business concerns, violating salt laws and forest laws, withholding payment of chaukidari taxes, rent and revenue, hoisting of Congress flags and holding of Congress sessions, using a secret radio transmitter in Bombay in August 1932 and a series of bombs—for a year and a half before admitting defeat.

It was in the midst of the civil disobedience that Ramsay MacDonald announced his Communal Award on 17 August 1932 providing separate electorates for Muslim, European and Sikh voters. There was to be a reservation of seats for women and provision for separate electorates for the Depressed Classes as a separate community. Gandhi who had been a great crusader against untouchability strongly opposed this scheme of separate electorates for the "Untouchables," now officially described as Scheduled Castes. On 18 August he informed MacDonald of his intention to commence fast unto death at noon on 20 September at Yeravda prison, Poona, till the scheme was revised and a common electorate restored. Gandhi's fast on 20 September which was observed as a day of prayers and fasting in India was able to secure an agreement between caste Hindus and untouchable leaders, after it entered on the fifth day, by which the Award was later modified. The Hindu joint electorate was retained with reserved seats for untouchables who were now given greater representation than before by MacDonald.

The Poona Pact of 25 September 1932, as it came to be known, was considered by many Congressmen as an unfortunate shifting of emphasis from the main object of the Civil Disobedience Movement. Nehru felt it to be a harmful diversion from the main task of a struggle against the British Raj: "I felt annoyed with him [Gandhi] for choosing a side issue for his final sacrifice. What would be the result on our freedom movement? Would not the larger issues fade into the back ground for the time being at least?" At the same time orthodox Hindus within the Congress like Malaviya, for example, who had been very close to Gandhi earlier now began to drift away. Gandhi's refusal to concern himself overmuch with other provisions of the Award which had given Muslims 49 percent of seats in the Punjab and 48.6 percent in Bengal sharpened their resentment against Gandhi.

Civil disobedience was gradually allowed to slip into the background and Harijan upliftment now became the principal concern of Gandhi. The shrewd British Raj found it advantageous to allow Gandhi to conduct Harijan work even from jail: an All-India Anti-Untouchability League was started in September 1932 and an weekly, *Harijan*, in January 1933. On 8 May Gandhi announced his intention to begin a fast of 21 days for purification of himself and his associates and for "greater vigilance and watchfulness in connection with the Harijan cause." The Raj released him to do this and immediately after his release Gandhi issued a long statement recommending to the Congress President suspension of civil disobedience for six weeks so that the whole purpose of the fast could not be frustrated. He also made an appeal to the Raj to withdraw the ordinance and release the civil disobedience prisoners, which, however, went unheeded.

By March 1933, according to an estimate of Malaviya, nearly 120,000 persons, among them quite a number of children and several thousand women including Gandhi's wife, Kasturba and mother of Jawaharlal Nehru were arrested and imprisoned. This indicates how strong was the will to continue civil disobedience. Yet in deference to Gandhi's wishes, the Acting President of the Congress, Aney, suspended the civil disobedience, at first for a period of six weeks and then for a further period of another six weeks. As soon as Gandhi recovered from the effects of the fast, he was requested by the Congress at Poona on 12 July 1923 "to seek an interview with the Viceroy for arriving at a settlement with the Government." When the interview was denied, the Congress decided to continue the struggle not in the form of mass civil disobedience but in the shape of individual civil disobedience. The flames of the movement had indeed died down now but the "burning embers" remained "for a long time hot and unquenchable as India's will to freedom." The movement was finally abandoned in April 1934.

Gandhi's cry for a temporary halt in May 1933 which did great damage to the movement was not criticised much in India as his earlier action in suspending the Non-Co-operation Movement after the Chauri Chaura incident, by his fellow Congressmen as they were too pre-occupied with the state of his health. Only Vithalbhai Patel and Subhas Chandra Bose who had then been far away from the Indian political scene could issue a manifesto from Vienna condemning Gandhi's decision to suspend the civil disobedience and stating that it virtually undid the work and sacrifice of the last thirteen years. The manifesto further pointed out that Gandhi's decision signified the failure of his leadership and the need for a more radical leader than Gandhi.

Bose and Vithalbhai Patel's open criticism of Gandhi after the suspension of the civil disobedience in May 1933 on an issue not directly relevant to the freedom movement signified the rise of a Left Wing which dominated the Congress in the years immediately after the passing of the Government of India Act of 1935.

Chapter 26

Act of 1935

Ramsay MacDonald followed up his announcement of Communal Award in August 1932 by summoning the third and final session of the Round Table Conference on 17 November which lasted till the end of December 1932. It was largely a small gathering of 46 delegates compared to the second session in 1931 which was attended by 112 delegates. The Congress which was then staging civil disobedience in India did not attend the session. The Conference was followed by the British Government issuing a White Paper in March 1933 and setting up a Joint Select Committee of Parliament, under Linlithgow, with a provision merely for consulting Indians. Quite naturally and expectedly many of the admittedly restricted concessions offered in 1930-31 under pressure of civil disobedience were now reduced through this process. And in August 1935, the Government of India Act emerged after a long and tortuous process which started eight years earlier with the appointment of the Simon Commission in 1927.

The Act was criticised by the Indian public opinion represented by the Congress, the Muslim League and the Liberals as indicating little advance over the reforms proposed in the Act of 1919. Spearheaded by Churchill with the support of Lancashire interests in India, the Tory pressure in the British Parliament throttled Indian hopes by substituting indirect for direct elections at the federal level and tightening up the machinery of official "discretionary powers," "reservations" and "safeguards."

In the Provincial sphere, Burma was separated from India and two new Provinces, Orissa and Sind, were created. Dyarchy was abolished and all the Provincial subjects were transferred to popular control in view of the Federal Form of Government envisaged at the Centre. The Governors were allowed certain "special responsibilities" as before. Bicameral Legislatures were established in Madras, Bombay, Bengal, the United Provinces, Bihar and Assam. The official blocs disappeared and the nomination of persons to represent backward classes and other interests ceased. There was no change in principle in the allocation of seats among the different communities as special interests. The Communal Award, as modified by the Poona Pact, regulated the distribution of seats among them. Property qualifications remained the main basis for enfranchisement. While a very much high standard was adopted for the Upper House, franchise for the Lower Houses was fixed at a much lower level than before with the result of more than four-fold increase in the number of voters.

In the Centre, the Federation of India was to be inaugurated only after the Rulers of the Indian States entitled to one-half of the seats allotted to them collectively in the Federal Upper Chamber had executed Instruments of Accession. As the country was considered not yet ready for the transfer of full responsibility at the Centre, dyarchic executive was provided for as was hitherto prevalent in the Provinces. However, the Federal Government as proposed in the Act never came into operation and there was no change in the Central Government as set up by the Act of 1919, except the establishment of a Federal Court, a Federal Public Service commission and a Federal Railway Authority.

Finally, the Act remained entirely silent about Dominion Status though nearly six years had elapsed after 1rwin's announcement of "the attainment of Dominion Status" to be "the natural issue of

India's constitutional progress" on 31October 1929. The hoax in such observation could be seen when Linlithgow, the Chairman of the Joint Select Committee, which drafted the Act, wrote as Viceroy of India in December 1939 to Zetland, the Secretary of State, nearly four years after the Act had come into existence: "The Act had been framed because we thought that way the best way of maintaining British influence in India. It is no part of our policy, I take it, to gratuitously to hurry the handing over the control to Indian hands to any pace faster than that which we regard as best calculated, on a long view, to hold India to the Empire."

Chapter 27

Revolutionaries Again

The years between the suspension of the Non-Co-operation Movement in February 1922 and the passing of the Government of India Act of 1935 were also the years which were marked by an intense revival of revolutionary activities. Newspapers, journals, periodicals and leaflets extolling revolutionary deeds and ideas reappeared and revolutionary groups like *Anushilan Samiti* and Yugantar Party in Bengal became active again.

In October 1924 a Conference of Revolutionaries was held in Lucknow and its outcome was an all-India organisation called Hindustan Republican Association—"to establish a federated Republic of the United States of India by an organised and armed revolution." One of the most daring acts of this Association led by very young Ramprasad Bismil was a dacoity in a railway train carrying the contents of the government treasury proceedings from Kakori towards Alamnagar, on 9 August 1925. The plot was discovered and suspects arrested by the police and a case was instituted which became known as the Kakori Conspiracy ease. Bismil was sentenced to death.

In September1928 at a meeting in the romantic setting of the ruins of Ferozeshah Kotla in Delhi, Bhagat Singh who had escaped after killing Saunders responsible for police lathi-charge on Lajpat Rai, and his Punjab group of Naujawan Bharat Sabha and Kirti

Kisan Party, Sachindranath Sanyal's brother Jatindranth and Ajoy Ghosh from the United Provinces and Phanindranath Ghosh from Bihar founded the Hindustan Socialist Republican Association. The Association believed that it was only the popular mass revolutionary action which would liberate India from colonial slavery. It gave the slogan: Revolution by the masses, for the masses and Long Live Revolution, that is, *Inquilab Zindabad.* The Association also believed that political explanatory work among the villagers was necessary and emphasised that the inevitable stage in the revolutionary struggle was terrorist acts of individual heroism and sacrifice which could only arouse the masses. Among the HSRA activists, Bhagat Singh was not only marked by an increasingly deep commitment to Marxian socialism but to militant atheism—which was clearly a great contrast with the strong Hindu religiosity of the earlier terrorists. The HSRA was organised with Central Committee and with Provincial and District Committees under it.

The HSRA made their appearance before the Indian people on 8 April 1929 when Bhagat Singh and Batukeshar Dutt threw a bomb from the visitors' gallery at the government benches which had just announced the promulgation of the special ordinances bringing into force the Trade Dispute Bill and Public Safety Amendment Bill. They also threw in the air copies of "Red Pamphlet." Their bomb was innocuous, they only wanted "to make the deaf hear" and they allowed themselves to be arrested so that they could use the court as a forum to explain their ideology to the people.

As a sequel to dropping of the bomb on the floor of the Legislative Assembly, the police discovered a bomb factory at Lahore and another at Saharanpur and instituted the Lahore Conspiracy Case against the revolutionaries arrested. The charges included murder, including the murder of Saunders earlier, conspiracy to wage war against the King and violation of Arms Act and Explosives Act. In the course of trial, the under-trial prisoners started a hunger strike claiming to be treated as war-prisoners and not as ordinary criminals as they had been charged with waging war against the King. While all the prisoners gave up the fast ultimately, Jatin Das stuck to it firmly and died after 64 days of fast on 13 September 1929. Nehru who went to see him in jail, found him "soft and gentle like a young girl." A large crowd gathered outside the jail gate to pay respect to Jatin who died heroically like the Irish revolutionary Terence McSwiney and the scene was repeated at all principal railway stations when it was conveyed by train to Calcutta where a two kilo meter long procession followed his bier.

The Lahore Conspiracy Case delivered its judgement through a Special Tribunal awarding capital punishment to Sukhdev, Rajguru and Bhagat Singh on 7 October 1930. In the course of his trial, Bhagat Singh, a young man of 23 only, had already explained that revolution for him was, "not the cult of the bomb and pistol" but a total change of society and no sacrifice was too great for so magnificent a cause—"we are content. We await the advent of revolution, Inquilab Zindabad." Now awaiting his execution in the concerned cell, Bhagat explained his total rejection of all religion on grounds of human dignity and rationalistic logic when he wrote a moving piece,—*Why I am an Atheist*.

The activities of the HSRA which included besides the murder of Saunders and the Assembly bomb, an attempt to blow up Irwin's train in Delhi in December 1929 were still continued by a handful of revolutionaries led by Chandrasekhar Azad till his death in a skirmish with the police at Allahabad in 1931.

While the daring deeds of the HSRA revolutionaries set all Northern India agog, there was also a boisterous revival of similar activities in Bengal. The most spectacular and daring among them was a raid on the government armouries at Chittagong on 18 April 1930 led by a veteran revolutionary, Surya Sen, popularly known as *Masterda*. A manifesto issued by Surya Sen in the name of the Indian Republican Army, Chittagong Branch, called on Indians to rise in war against the British. The news of his Chittagong raid led to terrorist activities in various parts of the country. Binoy, Badal and Dinesh raided the Writers' Building, Calcutta, on 8 December 1930 and assassinated the Inspector-General of Prisoners and some other British officials. Binoy and Badal committed suicide to evade arrest while Dinesh who was unsuccessful in similar suicide bid was arrested and later hanged by the British Raj. In 1932 fourteen of the accused in the Chittagong Armoury Raid Case were awarded transportation for life but Sen and four of his associates who had avoided arrest continued their activities for some time. On 22 September a group of young revolutioraries led by a young girl Pritilata Waddedar raided the Railway Institute at Pahartali in Chittagong. Pritilata committed suicide to evade arrest when she was seriously' injured. Surya sen was finally arrested in February 1933, through treachery and was hanged after trial.

These young revolutionaries did not believe in the principle of non-violence taught by Gandhian *Satyagraha*. Yet their patriotism, devotion and sacrifice earned the nation's respect and admiration. The passing of the Act of 1935 which provided for the establishment of the responsible government in the provinces seemed to take the wind out of the sail of the revolutionaries though sporadic acts of violence occurred often in the Punjab, Bengal, the United Provinces, Delhi and elsewhere.

Chapter 28

Congress and Congress Ministries

One year after the Act of 1935, the election of Nehru as President of the two successive Congress sessions in 1936—one in April at Lucknow and the other in December at Faizpur, demonstrated the rise of the Left Wing within the Congress. As a matter of fact, by 1936 the Congress had expanded from a humble elite organisation of 1885 to "become the largest organisation of the common people drawn very largely from the village population and counting among its members lakhs of peasants and cultivators and a sprinkling of industrial and field workers."

In his presidential address at Lucknow, Nehru said that he was convinced that "the only key to the solution of the world's problems and of India's problem lies in socialism, not in a vague humanitarian way but in the scientific economic sense." He welcomed the Soviet Union which had shown remarkable progress under the two Five Year Plans and was not affected by the great slump of 1929 as a "new civilization." And declared, "we who labour for a free India inevitably take our stand with the progressive forces of the world which are ranged against Fascism and Imperialism."

The two Congress sessions at Lucknow and Faizpur symbolised a new international perspective of our freedom movement in India when Nehru successfully pushed through them resolutions condemning Italian and Japanese aggression and expressing solidarity with Abyssinia, China and Republican Spain. In the Bombay Congress in October 1934 Gandhi had insisted on a reduction in the number of delegates, a Khadi qualification for Congress office-bearers and tighter control by the President and the Working Committee nominated by him—Nehru described this trend as "authoritarian" in the Congress organisation and suggested that it could be converted into a real anti-imperialist "joint popular front" by throwing its doors open to "corporate membership" of trade unions and Kisan Sabhas formed in India since the emergence of the Communist and Socialist ideas and activities in the mid-1920s among a group of disillusioned revolutionaries, Khilafatists and Non-Co-operators, like Narendranath Bhattacharji, better known as M.N. Roy, Abani Mukherjee, Virendranath Chattopadhyaya, Bhupenciranath Dutt, Mohammad Ali, Mohammad Shafiq, Barkatullah, S.A. Dange, Muzaffar Ahmad, Singaravelu and Ghulan Hussain. As a matter of fact, Nehru's Working Committee after Lucknow included three Socialists—they were Jayaprakash Narayan, Narendra Dev and Achyut Patwardhan. Nehru wanted to fight the elections which were to be held as per the provisions of the Act of 1935 on a radical programme which included a demand for a Constituent Assembly based on universal suffrage as well as the minimum demands of the Kisan Manifesto of All India Kishan Sabha which had asked for reductions in revenue and rent, agricultural income tax, fixity of tenure, scaling down of debts, end of forced labour, recognition of forest rights and of peasant unions.

No doubt that with such a radical agrarian programme the Congress was able to sweep the polls in elections held at the beginning of 1937 as the predominantly or general Hindu seats were concerned. The Muslim League desired to form a coalition government in each province but the Congress refused to admit into the ministry anyone who did not subscribe to its creed. The rejection vindicated the Congress stand that it was a national party under which all minorities interest was well-protected. However, it angered Jinnah who now declared: "Muslims can expect neither justice nor fair play under Congress Government." "From the classes" Jinnah now "went to masses with the cry of Islam in danger" and his sentiments were fully shared by the majority of Muslims who elected him every year as President of the Muslim League.

In seven out of eleven provinces—the Congress formed Ministries. Their programme of primary education, prohibition, uplift of the Harijans and rural reconstruction brought the Congress into the wider contact with the masses and the Congress grew in popularity. Within it also grew the growing influence of the younger section or the Left Wing whose socialist creed was not quite in tune with the orthodox views of Gandhi. Gandhi who had not been a primary member of the Congress at his own will since 1934 was "still the power behind the throne" and as Nehru had observed elsewhere, "the permanent Super-President of the Congress" or "the Congress at present meant Gandhiji." He attended on a standing invitation all the meetings of the Working Committee and the All India Congress Committee.

The Congress session at Haripura in Gujarat on 19 February 1938 saw the unanimous selection of Subhas Chandra Bose, the leader of the Left Wing in the Congress, as its President. The Haripura Congrees made it clear that independence must be for the whole of India, including the Indian States, the stronghold of British imperialism, bulwarks of feudal autocracy and exploitation, which had recently been affected by a people's liberation movement. As war clouds were gathering on the Western horizon, the Congress passed a long resolution condemning all war preparations and asserting that "India can be no party to such an imperialist war, and will not permit her manpower and resources to be exploited in the interests of British imperialism." Bose differed fundamentally from Gandhi on the subject of India's attitude towards the British Government during the forthcoming World War as well as on vital issues like the future course of the national movement and the industrial development of India for which as President of the Congress he had set up the National Planning Committee in late 1938.

In March 1939 Subhas Chandra Bose was again elected President of the Congress at Tripuri in the Central Provinces which adopted resolutions reiterating the Congress objective—achievement of independence, rejection of the Federation Part of the Act of 1935, "a Constituent Assembly, elected by the people on the basis of the adult franchise and without any interference by a foreign authority." The Congress further asserted the urgent need for India "to direct her foreign policy as an independent nation, thereby keeping aloof from both Imperialism and Fascism and pursuing her path of peace and freedom."

However, development within the Congress itself soon forced Bose's hands. After Haripura, Bose had not included a single Leftist, besides Nehru, in his Working Committee and had not done anything to prevent the development of an increasingly hostile attitude by the Congress Ministries towards labour and kisan militancy. Gandhi made his position more critical by declaring the defeat of his candidate by Bose in the Congress presidential election to be "more mine than his." On 22 February, 13 out of the 15 members of the old Working Committee resigned and at the March Tripuri Congress, Govinda Ballav Pant moved the famous resolution expressing confidence in the old Working Committee, reiterating faith in the Gandhian policies followed during the last twenty years, and asking Bose, almost incapacitated by illness, to nominate his Working Committee "in accordance with the wishes of Gandhiji." In April at the Calcutta session of the All India Congress Committee, Bose failed to take up Gandhi's challenge—"You are free to choose your own Committee"—because of disunity within the Left Wing and preferred to resign from the Congress presidentship and was succeeded by a staunch Gandhian Right Winger, Rajendra Prasad. In May 1939 Bose announced the formation of his Forward Bloc—"a radical and progressive party within the Congress, with a view to rallying the entire Left Wing under one banner." In June 1939 the Forward Bloc actually started a Left Consolidation Committee. But Bose's differences with the High Command were so fundamental that the Forward Bloc which was intended to be a party within a party came to have a separate identity by the end of August 1939.

While the Congress as a party was passing through these internal tensions, the Congress Ministries in the provinces were becoming counter-productive. The Ministries were increasingly facing the problem of alienation of workers, kisans and all Left elements within the party. At the same time, they were unable to please landlords or business groups when in the face of tight financial constraints of provincial autonomy, they took recourse to things like Bombay urban property tax. Such was the hopeless nature of the financial position of the Congress Ministries in the provinces that in July 1939 Vallabhbhai Patel hinted that the Ministries might have to resign unless the provinces received a greater share of income tax. Finally, they were also realising the embarrassing possibility of using the new emergency powers against demonstrations by their own party men if the war broke out soon.

The war was declared on 3 September 1939 by Britain on Germany and in the absence of the operation of the Federal Part of the Act of 1935, India as a colony of Britain was automatically committed to belligerency by Linlithgow without bothering to consult the Provincial Ministries or any Indian leader. Yet because of a very strong anti-Fascist feelings among the leaders, the immediate reaction of the Congress was conciliatory. The Working Committee meeting on 14 September 1939 invited "the British Government to declare in unequivocal terms what their war aims are in regard to democracy and imperialism and the new order that is envisaged; in particular, how these aims are going to apply to India and to be given effect to in the present."

Linlithgow took more than a month to tell the Congress on 17 October his inability to elaborate the war aims of Britain further than the British Prime Minister. As for the immediate present, he was prepared to include more Indians in the Executive Council and it was only after the war, various groups and sections would be consulted to see what modifications were necessary in the Act of 1935 so that "India may attain her due place among the great Dominions."

From the Congress point of view, the Viceroy's reply was far from satisfactory. Britain was not only unwilling to part with power at the moment but also to grant complete independence after the war. The Working Committee rejected Linlithgow's offer and asked the Congress Ministries in the provinces to resign on 29-30 October, which they did.

Chapter 29

Towards Freedom

In the annual session at Ramgarh in March 1940, the Congress presided over by Maulana Abul Kalam Azad while reaffirming the demand for complete independence, was alarmed at the runaway victories of the Germans. Contrary to the ideas of Bose who believed that "only after the defeat and breakup of the British Empire could India hope to be free," Gandhi wrote: "We do not seek independence out of Britain's ruin" and Nehru reasserted his anti-Fascist stand: "India is completely opposed to the idea of the triumph of Nazism." So at the instance of C.Rajagopalachari the Congress modified its demand for complete independence and offered to co-operate with the British Government provided a provisional National Government was set up at the Centre.

The British Raj's response to the Congress offer of co-operation came in the form of a statement by Linlithgow on 8 August 1940. He offered to set up a representative body to devise a new constitution after the war, to enlarge his Executive Council by nominating additional Indian members and to appoint a "War Advisory Council" consisting of representatives of the British India and the Indian States—almost a repetition of his 17 October 1939 stand. The Congress proposal to set up a Provisional National Government was turned down as the British Government "could not contemplate the transfer of their present responsibilities for the peace and welfare of India to any system of Government whose authority is directly denied by large and powerful elements in India's national life."

This explanation of the British decline of the Congress proposal was intended to assure the Muslim League which was claiming itself to be the sole representative organisation of the Muslims that no constitution be framed without its consent and approval. In the early years of the war, the Muslim League, while remaining firm in its attitude of non-co--operation, offered co-operation with the British Government on its acceptance of "the two-nation theory" demanding a separate state for Muslims, the idea of which could be traced to such observations of Muhammed Iqbal, the well-known poet, as in 1930 when he said "Muslims demand for the creation of a Muslim India." The idea of a separate state for Muslims received further impetus when Rahamat Ali belonging to a group of young Muslim students at Cambridge conveyed to the Muslim delegates at the time of the Round Table Conference in London the scheme of a separate Muslim homeland consisting of the Punjab, Afghan Province or North-West Frontier Province, Kashmir, Sind and Baluchistan. The name of the new homeland, Pakistan, meaning, Sacred Land, was to be derived by taking the first letter of the first four provinces and the end of the last named province. The Muslim delegates dismissed the scheme as "only a student's scheme" which was "chimerical and impracticable." However, Rahamat Ali did not give up the idea, founded the Pakistan National Movement in 1933 to propagate it and by 1940 it was hotly catching up with the Muslim leaders when the Muslim League declared in March 1940 that Muslims in India must have a separate independent state. The August offer by the British Raj to the Congress, though not completely satisfactory to the League, certainly allayed their fears of a Congress Raj in India.

The August offer was, however, totally unacceptable to the Congress. The Raj's attitude to the minority problem particularly irked it. As Nehru wrote: "It is the old language of imperialism and the content has changed in no way." So in October 1940 the

Congress started an individual civil disobedience under Gandhi. One of the first persons to offer individual *Satyagraha* was Acharya Vinobha Bhave, specially selected by Gandhi. The futility of such a campaign was recognised by many and even, Congressmen who had suffered imprisonment for it joined with them in an appeal to Gandhi to call it off. However, Gandhi would neither withdraw it nor convert it into a mass movement as a large section of people desired, for he feared that the mass action during the war would embarrass the British Government. And the movement was continued "without much enthusiasm on the part of Gandhi and his followers."

In August 1941, all sections of Indians heartily welcomed the "Atlantic Charter" jointly issued by U.K. and U.S.A. as a statement of their war policy, which declared, among other things that "they respect the right of all peoples to choose the form of government under which they will live, and they wish to see sovereign rights and self-government restored to those who have been forcibly deprived of them." However, the hopes raised by the Charter among Indians were short-lived as Churchill clarified in the House of Commons on 9 September 1941 that "the Atlantic Charter" had no application to India though, in his opinion, it was in full accord with the British policy in India, as embodied in the August offer of 1940. Churchill's statement in the House of Commons clearly exposed the British policy which never wanted to make any real constitutional concession to Indians.

In December 1941, the course of the war took a dramatic turn for the worse after Japan had joined the Axis camp with its bombing of Pearl Harbour. Linlithgow now made a public appeal for a united national front. The Congress renewed its offer to co-operate with the British Government on condition that India be granted full independence. As has been aptly observed, "The country wanted freedom before victory, the government victory before freedom." The fall of Singapore on 15 February 1942 followed by the fall of Rangoon on 7 March brought home to everyone including the

U.S.A. President, Roosevelt, the danger to India. Roosevelt took a more realistic view of the whole situation and urged upon Churchill, who could not ignore Roosevelt, as Britain's safety threatened with a Nazi attack depended upon the American help, to settle matters with India to resist Japanese advance. The British Government decided to send to India Sir Stafford Cripps, a Labour Member of the British War Cabinet under Churchill who had earlier privately visited India in December 1939, to survey the situation and find out the solution after consultation with the Indian leaders. The very day, 11 March 1942, on which Churchill announced the Cripps Mission, Roosevelt appointed Louis A. Johnson, formerly his Assistant Secretary of War, to be his personal representative at Delhi during the period of Cripps Mission.

Sir Stafford Cripps arrived at Delhi on 23 March with a Draft Declaration approved by the British War Cabinet. Declaring the aim of the British Government to be "the earliest possible realisation of self-government in India," the Draft Declaration promised Dominion Status with right of secession from the British Commonwealth and "a constitution making body" elected by provincial legislatures, with the individual provinces being given the right not to join it, and with the Indian States being invited to appoint representatives. The Draft Declaration also invited "immediate and effective participation of the leaders of the principal sections of the Indian people in the counsels of their country" on urgent issues except "the control and the direction of the defence of India" which the British would retain during the war.

The Congress was naturally very critical and suspicious of the clauses relating to nominating of representatives by rulers of Indian States and provincial option which according to the private admission of Amery, the Secretary of State was to be "the first public admission of the possibility of Pakistan." However, the proposals which alienated the rest of India failed to satisfy the Muslims whom they were intended to conciliate. The Muslim League demanded "a definite pronouncement in favour of partition," and declined to participate in a constitution making body not "elected by separate electorates." Driven by his own sincere desire for a settlement in his talks with the official Congress negotiators, Nehru and Maulana Abul Kalam Azad, Cripps perhaps went beyond "the limits" of the Draft Declaration. A War Cabinet telegram to Cripps on 9 April sharply pulled him up for not adequately consulting Linlithgow and the Commander-in-Chief, Wavell and giving Johnson, Roosevelt's representative, too much scope. It also deplored "allusions to a National Government" and emphasised the need "to bring the whole matter back to Cabinet's plan which you went out to urge." The same evening of 9 April the Congress negotiators found Cripps singing a completely different tune—for example, Cripps clarified by "a National Government" he meant an expansion of the Viceroy's Executive Council—and the talks broke down abruptly.

The Cripps Mission failed because Churchill was not much interested in arriving at a settlement despite his pretensions to show to the world that he was sincerely interested in it. On 11 April he warmly congratulated Cripps' efforts as proving "how great was the British desire to reach a settlement." Cripps blamed the Congress for the failure to save his future political career. There is, however, little doubt that except Nehru who had desperately sought a settlement to mobilize genuine and effective Indian support in developing "a blazing fire of resistance," as he wrote to Roosevelt on 12 April, "which no aggressor could have faced successfully," most Congress Working Committee members and Gandhi himself had been apathetic or cynical from the beginning. Gandhi who had deliberately kept himself very much in the background throughout the period of Cripps' stay in India described the long-term proposals of Cripps for the future constitution of India as a "post-dated cheque on a crashing bank."

Gandhi's indifference to the Cripps' Mission could possibly be explained with reference to a change in the attitude of co-operation that he had been developing over the past few months. British withdrawal from Malaya, Singapore, Burma, Philippines and Indonesia following a strategy of "defence in depth" with its scorched earth policy had ravaged the countries wholesale. A taste of what the future held for India was available when thousands of small river boats in Bengal were destroyed to prevent them from falling into the hands of the advancing Japanese, thereby seriously affecting the distribution of food supplies in Bengal, criss-crossed by rivers, large and small. Immediately after the failure of the Cripps' Mission to arrive at a settlement, Gandhi wrote in the *Harijan* on 19 April 1942 suggesting that the safety and interest of both Britain and India "lie in orderly and timely British withdrawal from India." This puzzled Nehru who held very strongly that in any case India must fight with Britain against Fascism.

Inspite of the compromise and almost non-committal resolution of the Congress Working Committee at Allahabad, 20 April—2 May 1942, Gandhi wrote a series of articles elaborating his idea which was soon to crystallise into the "Quit India" Movement. In early May he wrote: "The presence of British in India is an invitation to Japan to invade India. Their withdrawal removes the bait. Assume, however, it does not; free India will be better able to cope with the invasion. Unadulterated non-co-operation will then have full sway." On 24 May he further explained: "Let them [British] entrust India to God or in modern parlance to anarchy. Then all the parties will fight one another like dogs, or will, when the real responsibility faces them, come to a reasonable agreement. I shall expect non-violence to arise out of the chaos."

Gandhi's hard line was backed by a combination of Right Wingers like Patel, Prasad and Kripalani and Socialists like Achyut Patwardhan and Narendra Dev, while Nehru found himself in the strange company of the arch-Moderates like Rajagopalachari and Bhulabhai Desai. On 14 July the Congress Working Committee which met at Wardha adopted a resolution demanding immediate end of the British rule in India as it was "necessary not only in the interest of India but also for the safety of the world and for the ending of Nazism, Fascism, militarism, and the aggression of one nation against another." The resolution proposed to set up a Provisional Government and to convene the Constituent Assembly to draft a constitution for India after the withdrawal of the British. It however clearly asserted that the Congress had no sympathy for the aggressive designs of Japan or any other power associated with the Axis group and was therefore "agreeable to the stationing of the armed forces of the Allies in India in order to ward off and resist Japanese or other aggression." If this appeal failed, the resolution asserted, the Congress would be then "reluctantly compelled to utilise all the non-violent strength it might have gathered since 1920, when it adopted non-violence as part of its policy for the vindication of political rights and liberty. Such a widespread struggle would inevitably be under the leadership of Gandhiji."

The resolution which was to be endorsed by an AICC meeting kept the option for negotiations open. Mira Ben, one of Gandhi's staunch disciples went to Delhi, to meet the Viceroy in order to apprise him of the purport of the resolution of 14 July and the nature of the movement proposed by it. The Viceroy made it clear that the Government of India would not tolerate any rebellion, violent or non-violent, during the war and refused to meet Mira Ben to discuss the issue. In England, the attempts of Chiang Kai-Shek of China and President Roosevelt of the United States, to persuade Britain to come to terms with India were answered by a public declaration of Churchill that he had not "become His Majesty's first minister to preside over the liquidation of the British Empire."

On 7 August the All India Congress Committee met in Bombay and on 8 August, after prolonged discussions, passed a resolution endorsing the resolution of 14 July and deciding to start "a mass struggle on non-violent lines on the widest possible scale" under the leadership of Gandhi and made a passionate appeal to all Indian nationalists to join the movement which would lead "ultimately to the independence and deliverance of India." The "Quit India" resolution which was moved by Nehru who had swallowed his doubts as before was opposed only by the arch-Moderates like Rajagopalachari, who was willing to accept Cripps' plan and Bhulabhai Desai who had resigned in July. After the resolution was passed, the Committee members heard Gandhi with rapt attention: "Everyone of you should from this moment onwards consider yourself a free man or woman and act as if you are free. I am not going to be satisfied with anything short of complete freedom. We shall do or die. We shall either free India or die in the process."

Promptly came the iron hands which were determined to throttle the movement before it started. Within a few hours of his address to the Committee members, Gandhi along with all Congress leaders, was arrested in the early morning hours of 9 August, the Congress headquarters at Allahabad were seized and Congress funds confiscated.

The news of the arrest of Gandhi and other Congress leaders was immediately followed by non-violent popular demonstrations in the shape of hartals and processions all over India. Since all the Congress leaders who mattered were in jail, there was no one to guide the masses and the movement no longer remained non-violent—it developed into a violent defiance of the British Raj. Symbols of British Raj like police stations, post offices, railway stations were attacked, set on fire and wrecked. Telegraph and telephone wires were cut, railway lines damaged and barricades in cities and towns raised. Peasants were continuously exhorted not to pay taxes to the British Raj. In many places like Tamluk in Bengal, Satara in Bombay, Ballia in the United Provinces, and Talcher in Orissa, parallel governments were set up. And as before, the leading part was played by the students. The Congress Socialists like Jayaprakash Narayan, Ram Manohar Lohia and Aruna Asaf Ali joined the movement though the Communists now freed from the ban since 1934 following a wide strike of textile workers stayed away from it. Besides the Communists, the Muslim League, as was expected, kept itself aloof from the movement and together with the Depressed Classes denounced it. Apart from applying the provisions of the Defence of India Act, the British Raj took other stern measures like firing from aeroplanes. According to the official estimates, more than 60,000 people were arrested, 18,000 detained without trial, 940 killed, and 1,630 injured through police or military firing during the last five months of 1942. In the face of such large scale heavy repression, the movement soon began to show signs of decline after giving burst, in a striking and unmistakable manner, to India's hatred and anger against British Raj and her determination to be free from the imperial clutches.

As the Quit India Movement withered, the Raj was soon faced with an external danger. The June 1942 Bangkok Conference of the Indian Independence League set up by Rashbehari Bose in Japan decided to organise the Indian prisoners of war into an Indian National Army, *Azad Hind Fauz*. In response to an invitation for the Bangkok Conference, Subhas Chandra Bose who had escaped to Germany in 1941, came to Tokyo in June 1943 and held discussions with the Japanese authorities who promised the independence of India after the war. Bose then came to Singapore, took over the leadership of the Indian National Army as Netaji and gave the famous war cry: "Chalo Delhi" or march on to Delhi. He inaugurated the Provisional Government of Free India at Singapore, chalked out a master plan of campaign with the ultimate goal of driving the British out of India. In 1943 his soldiers advanced with the Japanese army upto the very frontier of India and by March 1944 the Indian National Flag was unfurled in Kohima at a time when every where the Axis powers were in retreat. Between March and June 1944, the Indian National Army which included a women's detachment named after the Rani of Jhansi was in action on Indian soil, besieging Imphal along with the Japanese troops in a campaign which failed ultimately. The Japanese collapse next year made the Indian National Army men prisoners again while Bose disappeared mysteriously, alleged to have died in an air crash which some Indians still do not believe to be true.

The change in the international situation necessitated a change in the Congress policy. Gandhi who was imprisoned in the Aga Khan Palace in Poona was released on grounds of ill-health in May 1944 by Wavell who had succeeded Linlithgow as the Viceroy in October 1943. Gandhi realised that no solution of the Indian problem was possible without the concurrence of the Muslim League. Jinnah turned down Rajagoplachari's proposal as offering "a shadow and a husk, a maimed, mutilated and moth-eaten Pakistan" but agreed to discuss the matter with Gandhi. In September 1944 the two leaders met in Bombay and held discussions for a fortnight. Gandhi offered to accept the principle of Pakistan and urged the Muslim League, to join hands with the Congress in demanding immediate independence and pleaded for a Congress-League Provisional Government during the period of transition. Jinnah turned down the proposals asserting that partition must come before freedom. However, the break-down of talks, between Gandhi and Jinnah, did not prevent growing co-operation between the League and the Congress in the Central Assembly and the spread of strong rumours in January 1945 of an agreement between the two Assembly leaders, Liaquat Ali Khan and Bhulabhai Desai, by which the League and the Congress would form coalitions in the Centre and the Provinces under the existing conditions as war-time measures.

With elections round the corner, the British Raj took an initiative in breaking "the political deadlock in India." In March 1945 Wavell flew to London and came back with a plan which he announced on 14 June 1945. The plan, while reiterating the Cripps' offer of 1943, "in its entirety without change or qualification," stated that the members of the Vicerory's Executive Council, with the exception of the Vicerory and the Commander-in Chief, should be Indians selected from amongst the leaders of Indian political parties, on a basis of parity between Muslims and the so called caste Hindus. Amery commented: "We are placing India's immediate future in Indian hands." Wavell summoned a Conference of Indian political leaders at Simla on 25 June 1945 to select the personnel. Jinnah obstinately insisted that all the Muslim members of the Council must be from his Muslim League. Such a proposition was totally unacceptable to the Congress. As the chief spokesman of the Congress in the Conference, Maulana Abul Kalam Azad, pointed out that the Congress could not possibly be a party to any arrangement, however temporary it might be, that prejudiced its national character, tended to impair the growth of nationalism and reduced Congress directly or indirectly to a "communal body." The Simla talks broke down. The failure of the Conference, however, immensely strengthened the position of the Muslim League which could make or mar the constitutional progress of India as the Raj gave it the power to veto any constitutional proposal it did not like. The League increasingly attracted the "wavering and middle-of-the road Muslim politicians" as through it only they could reach the positions of power and profit.

In July 1945 the Labour won a massive victory. Wavell recorded in his *Viceroy's Journal* that the Labour Government might try to hand over "India to their friends as soon as possible" and it might become necessary for him to shift from the "accelerator" to the "brake pedal gently but firmly." He realised that though many of the Labour leaders were "in reality imperialists" who "like everyone else" hated "the idea of our leaving India" had "no alternative to suggest" like everyone else in the changing perspective worldwide, as well as Indian.

Indeed the international perspective had undergone tremendous change. In Europe, Nazi Germany had been destroyed and in Asia Japan had surrendered after Hiroshima in August 1945. Socialist regimes under Communist leadership or influence were emerging throughout Eastern Europe and were about to do so in France and Italy. In Asia the Chinese revolution was forging ahead, and a tremendous anti-imperialist wave was sweeping through South-East Asia where Vietnam and Indonesia were resisting French and Dutch efforts to restore their colonial rule. With a war-weary army and people and a ravaged economy, there is no doubt that Britain would have to retreat from India. The Labour Victory in July 1945 only quickened the process of retreat.

The first thing that Wavell did after the Labour Government had been installed in London was to announce on 21 August new elections in the coming winter as the "first step" towards providing "constitutional activities for the agitators" and thereby keeping them occupied. The last elections for the Centre had been held in 1934 and for the Provinces in 1937. After a brief visit to London, Wavell made a policy broadcast on 19 September by reiterating the promise of "early realisation of full self-government." A "Constitution-making body" would set up after the elections with members of the Legislative Assemblies and Indian States and efforts to set up an Executive Council "which will have the support of the main Indian parties" would be renewed.

The Congress and the Muslim League began to make hectic preparations for the coming elections in the winter of 1945-46. In the midst of these the British Raj initially decided to hold public trials of several hundred of the 20,000 Indian National Army prisoners on charges of treason. The Raj compounded the folly of holding the first trial in the Red Fort in Delhi in November 1945, and putting on the dock together a Hindu (P.K. Sehgal), a Muslim (Shah Nawaz Khan) and a Sikh (Gurbaksh Singh Dhillon). Jawaharlal Nehru who put on his barrister's gown after 25 years, Bhulabhai Desai and Tejbahadur Sapru appeared for the defence. The trials stirred the people emotionally and the Muslim League also joined the country wide protest. An intelligence Bureau Report admitted on 20 November that the trials had attracted tremendous Indian public interest and sympathy which "cut across communal barriers." The British Raj became extremely nervous about the sympathy spreading to the Indian army which it actually did in the

Punjab in January 1946 when a Lahore reception for the released prisoners of the Indian National Army was attended by Indian soldiers in uniform.

In the wake of the trials of the Indian National Army prisoners, there took place the naval mutiny in Bombay on 18 February 1946 when ratings in the Signals training establishment Talwar went on hunger-strike against bad food and racist insults and next day the strike spread to Castle and Fort Barracks on shore and twenty two ships anchored in Bombay harbour. The men were persuaded to withdraw their strike on the afternoon of 20 February only to find themselves surrounded by army men. Fighting started next day at Castle Barracks when ratings attempted to break out of their encirclement under cover of artillery support provided by the ships. Admiral Godfrey threatened to destroy the navy with the help of bombers. By 22 February 78 ships including some on sea, 20 shore establishments and 20,000 ratings were affected by the mutiny. However, Vallabhbhai Patel of the Congress and Jinnah of the Muslim League managed to persuade the ratings, Hindus and Muslims, to surrender on 23 February with an assurance that the national parties would prevent their victimization—an assurance they hardly found time to keep following immediate occurrence of important developments on the national scene which kept them occupied fully.

Chapter 30

Freedom at Midnight

One such immediate and important development was the holding of elections for the Central and the Provincial Legislative Assemblies. In view of Wavell's September 1945 announcement of early realisation of full self-government, these elections had assumed tremendous significance and the Congressmen had kept themselves fully pre-occupied with their preparations for them. As in 1937, Nehru was the star speaker and vote catcher while Patel controlled the election machinery. The Congress won in general constituencies routing its rivals—the Hindu Mahasabha and the Communists. In the Central Assembly the Congress captured 57 out of 102 seats against 36 in 1934 and in the provinces it won majorities everywhere except Bengal, Sind and the Punjab. The Muslim League also achieved spectacular success in the Muslim seats when it won all the 30 reserved constituencies in the Central Assembly and 442 out of 509 Muslim seats in the Provincial Assemblies. Yet a clear majority still eluded the Muslim League in the Punjab where Khizar Hayat Khan was able to strike a bargain with the Congress and the Akalis to remain in power for another year. In the two other provinces—North West Frontier Province and Assam now being claimed for Pakistan—the Congress won handsome majorities and the two League Ministries that came into existence in Bengal and Sind were able to do so with official and European support there.

The Labour Prime Minister, Clement Attlee, who was a member of the Simon Commission in 1927-28, announced in the House of Commons on 19 February 1946 that three members of his Cabinet— Lord Pethick Lawrence (the Secretary of State for India), Sir Stafford Cripps (now President of the Board of Trade) and A.V. Alexander (First Lord of the Admiralty), —would visit India soon "to promote, in conjunction with the leaders of Indian opinion, the early realisation of full self-government in India." The Congress hopes were further raised on 15 March when Attlee made a statement in the House of Commons promising speedy and full freedom and declaring that "though mindful of the rights of minorities, we cannot allow a minority to place their veto on the advance of the majority."

The Cabinet Mission came to Delhi on 24 March 1946 and began holding a series of conferences with the leaders of the Congress and the League. Wavell was very suspicious of the Cabinet Mission being over-friendly with the Congress. However, this was not solely due either to Labour Party's pro-nationalist sympathies or Cripps' old ties with Nehru but also to what Wavell himself admitted in his *Viceroy's Journal* on 29 March, "the necessity to avoid the mass movement or revolution which it is in the power of the Congress to start and which we are not certain that we can control." When the initial negotiations seemed to be stalled as usual on the rock of Jinnah's insistence on Pakistan, the Cabinet Mission on 16 May confronted him with a choice between a "moth-eaten" Pakistan and a loose, three-tier confederal structure in which Muslim would have the chance of dominating the North West and North East Provinces of a still united country. A full-fledged Pakistan was impossible since it would include a very large number of Non-Muslims and a partition of Bengal and the Punjab would go against deep-seated regional ties, raised any number of economic, administrative and military problems and still failed to satisfy the League. The alternative three-tier confederal structure suggested by the Cabinet Mission consisted of a weak Centre with control over foreign affairs, defence and communications only and of the existing Provincial Assemblies being grouped into three sections while electing the Constituent Assembly. Thus Section A would be for the Hindu-majority provinces, Sections B and C for the Muslim-majority provinces of the North West and North East which included Assam. All these Sections would have the power to set up their own intermediate level executives and legislatures. The Muslim League argued for compulsory grouping of the Sections so that Sections B and C could develop into solid entities with a view to future secession into Pakistan. The Congress which was critical of the absence of any provision for elected members from the Princely Indian States in the proposed Constituent Assembly argued that compulsory grouping of Sections contradicted the oft-repeated insistence on provincial autonomy. It also failed to satisfy itself that despite the compulsory grouping of Sections at first, the provinces would have the right to opt out after new elections held under the new constitution emerging out of the proposed Constituent Assembly.

Jinnah hoped that the Congress would reject the plan which the Muslim League had accepted on 6 June, and the British Raj would ask the League to form the Interim Government at the Centre—a hope fully shared by Wavell, who was deeply disappointed when the Congress accepted the long-term proposals on 24 June, just five days before the Cabinet Mission left India. Nehru, as the new President of the Congress, declared at a press conference on 10 July that the only commitment which his party had made by accepting the long-term proposals was to participate in the Constituent Assembly elections. He hoped that there would be "no grouping" since North West Frontier Province and Assam would have objections to joining Sections B and C. The Muslim League responded on 29-30 July by withdrawing its earlier acceptance of the long-term plan and calling on the "Muslim Nation" to go in for "Direct Action" on 16 August to achieve Pakistan. The day passed off almost peacefully in most parts of the country except in Calcutta which witnessed a shocking outburst of communal frenzy. The city and its suburbs had a terrible blood bath known as the "Great Calcutta Killing." For the next few days, large scale murders, mob attacks, arson and pillage went on unchecked with the connivance of the League Ministry in Bengal.

Wavell who after his failure to set up a short-term coalition Interim Government at the Centre had set up on 4 July a Caretaker Government of officials increasingly felt the need of somehow getting the Congress into it even if the League stayed out, to "control unruly elements," including "the Communists and their own Left Wing"—a view which was also shared by Patel. His attempt, however, to bully the Congress into accepting compulsory grouping of Sections was firmly resisted by Gandhi and Nehru on 27 August and Pethik-Lawrence advised Wavell in a "panic-stricken telegram" to avoid any break. On 2 September 1946 Nehru and his colleagues were sworn in as members of the Viceroy's Executive Council. Soon after this, the Hindus of a number of villages in the Noakhali district and the adjoining part of Comilla suffered terribly from the armed raids organised by Muslims and this provoked reprisals in Bihar, where large numbers of Muslims received the same treatment at the hands of Hindus. Nehru flew to Bihar where the Congress Ministry took vigourous steps to suppress the disturbances while Gandhi's peace mission in the affected areas had a sobering effect on the fratricidal fights.

Under Nehru's guidance, the Viceroy's Executive Council worked like a Cabinet. Wavell who found his power much reduced now decided to bring in the League members as a counterpoise in the name of communal parity. After telling Nehru that the League had agreed to join the Constituent Assembly, he reconstituted the Executive Council by including Muslim League members. This destroyed the team spirit of the Council as the League members openly repudiated the idea of collective responsibility. What was worse, the League announced that it would not participate in the

Constituent Assembly which was due to meet on 9 December 1946 and Jinnah made the startling disclosure much to the embarrassment of Wavell that it had never agreed to do so. The Secretary of State convened in London a meeting of the representatives of the parties concerned to find a way out of the baffling situation. The outcome of this was, as expected, not an agreement but an announcement by the British Government on 6 December 1946 that it would not implement any constitution drafted by a Constituent Assembly unrepresented by a large section of the people, as far as the Muslim-majority provinces were concerned. This announcement elated the Muslim League members and Jinnah now found himself in a very favourable position to clinch the issue in favour of Pakistan.

The Constituent Assembly met on 9 December 1946, as scheduled, without the members of the Muslim League. Rajendra Prasad was elected President and various committees were formed to draft the different parts of the constitution. The Congress now demanded the resignation of the Muslim League members from the Interim Government as the Muslim League was boycotting the Constituent Assembly and threatened to withdraw its own members from the government if the demand was not met, while the Muslim League from outside continued to press its demand for Pakistan. The country was thus passing though a tense period of suspense, fear and expectation while Gandhi, now an old man of 77, in December 1946 and January 1947, with a handful of companions and with undiminished courage and determination, was moving through the riot affected areas of Noakhali, Bihar and Calcutta, to vindicate his life-long principles of change of heart and non-violence.

It was in this context that Attlee announced in the House of Commons on 20 February the decision to quit India, fixing June 1948, as a dead-line for transfer of power. Attlee explained that if Indian politicians had not agreed by that date on a constitution, still the British would relinquish power "whether as a whole to some form of Central Government for British India, or in some areas to the existing Provincial Governments, or in such other way as may seem most reasonable and in the best interests of the Indian people." British powers and obligations towards the Indian States which would also cease with transfer of power would not, however, be passed on to any government that would succeed the British Raj. Attlee clearly hinted at the idea of partition and Balkanization of India into numerous states. Attlee's statement of 20 February 1947 were prompted by such practical considerations as were revealed by Cripps in the House of Commons debates on it. Cripps pointed out that the only alternative to the question of withdrawal from India was to continue to hold it on by total repression which meant stationing of large numbers of British troops in India for years. The people of Britain—"short as we are of manpower, as we all know"—would not have consented to an arrangement which "would be politically impracticable, from both a national and international point of view and would arouse the most. bitter animosity of all parties in India against us."

Attlee replaced Wavell by Mountbatten as the Viceroy of India who came to Delhi on 24 March 1947 to arrange for transfer of power. Attlee's pronouncement on 20 February 1947 had evoked hearty enthusiasm all over India. The Congress found the bait of complete transfer of power at an early date even at the cost of partition and possibly Balkanization too tempting to refuse in the context of increasing communal riots and growing Left menace both within and outside the party. The Muslim League took recourse to "Direct Action" in the wake of Attlee's statement to vindicate its demands for Pakistan. Wide areas of the Punjab and the North West Frontier Provinces became scenes of ugly riots and a large section of the Hindus and the Sikhs who had hitherto been strongly in favour of a united India now gradually came to realise its impracticability, and demanded partition of the Punjab and Bengal if the Muslim League refused to join the Constituent Assembly.

Mountbatten proceeded with his task at a break-neck speed. After a rapid series of 133 interviews with political leaders between 24 March and 6 May, he found that the Cabinet Mission Plan was no longer tenable and formulated his own plan which he code-named, "Plan Balkan." The Plan envisaged transfer of power to separate provinces including Bengal and the Punjab where the Legislative Assemblies were given the options to vote for partition of their provinces. The various units thus formed including the Indian States which would become independent by the lapse of British Paramountcy would then have the choice of joining India, Pakistan or remaining separate. In Simla on 10 May when Mountbatten informed Nehru privately about it, Nehru violently objected to it and the "Plan Balkan" was quickly abandoned in place of one which involved transfer of power to two Central Governments, India and Pakistan, on the basis of the grant of Dominion Status. The Plan now taken up was originally suggested by V.P. Menon, a very senior bureaucrat who played a key role in 1946-47 as confidante of Vallabhabhai Patel and trusted adviser of Wavell and Mountbatten, to the Secretary of State for India in January 1947. Patel had privately agreed with Menon's idea which formally meant for the Congress a retreat from the Lahore resolution of December 1929, since Dominion Status would ensure not only peaceful and quick transfer of power but win for India influential friends in Britain and allow for some continuity in the bureaucracy and the army.

Mountbatten who had been informally given much greater powers to decide things on the spot than his predecessors by the British Government announced the Plan on 3 June 1947 simultaneously with the British Prime Minister, Attlee, who announced it in the House of Commons. The next day, 4 June 1947, Mountbatten announced that transfer of power would be probably effected around 15 August 1947. The following were the main features of his Plan: First, if the areas with a majority of Muslim population so desired, they should be allowed to form a separate Dominion, and a new Constituent Assembly would be set up for the purpose. In that case there would be a partition of Bengal and the Punjab if the representatives of the Hindu majority districts in the Legislatures of those provinces so desired. Secondly, there would be a referendum in the North-West Frontier Province to ascertain whether it should join Pakistan or not. Thirdly, there would also be a referendum in the district of Sylhet to ascertain whether it should join Pakistan or not. Fourthly, Boundary Commissions would be set up to define the boundaries of the Hindu and the Muslim Provinces in Bengal and the Punjab. Finally, legislation would be introduced in the current session of the British Parliament for immediately conferring Dominion Status on India or the two Dominions if partition were decided upon, without any prejudice to the final decision of the Constituent Assembly or Assemblies in this respect.

The Mountbatten Plan was received with mixed feelings by the Indian people. The vivisection of India was an extremely bitter pill to swallow for many who had so long struggled with the idea of secular nationalism and an united Indian nation. The Congress accepted the plan not without any demurs. Nor was the Muslim League fully satisfied with the "truncated and moth-eaten Pakistan." In the North West Frontier Province, Abdul Ghaffar Khan and his Red Shirts whose demand for a separate independent state, Pakhtoonistan, was turned down by the British Government at the suggestion of Jinnah, were opposed to the decision concerning their province.

The Indian Independence Bill which was introduced in the British Parliament on 1 July 1947 was passed without any dissent and after receiving the assent of the king became an Act on 18 July. The Partition of Bengal and the Punjab was effected by two Commissions, each consisting of two nominees of the Congress and two of the Muslim League. Both the Commissions which were appointed by the British Government were chaired by Sir Cyril Radcliffe. The plebiscite in Sylhet district went in favour of joining

Pakistan by a majority vote while the Red Shirts in the North West Frontier Province boycotted the referendum which also went in favour of joining Pakistan. By 15 August 1947, all the Indian States except Kashmir, Junagadh and Hyderabad had agreed to sign, largely through the initiative of Patel, an Instrument of Accession with India or in a few cases like Bahawalpur with Pakistan, acknowledging Central authority over defence, external affairs and communications. The Princes agreed to this arrangement fairly easily for so far they were "surrendering" only what they never possessed—the three functions had been part of the British Paramountcy—and as yet there was no change in internal political structures.

Jinnah, as President of the Pakistan Constituent Assembly created on 11 August, was to become the Governor General of the Dominion of Pakistan comprising Sind, Baluchistan, the North-West Frontier Province, the West Punjab and the East Bengal. The Congress requested Mountbatten to continue to act as the Governor-General of the Dominion of India which included "a truncated" Bengal as well as the Punjab. For many Hindus in Pakistan and Muslims in India independence came to mean a cruel choice between threat of sudden violence and squeezing of employment and other economic opportunities or a forcible tearing out of age-old roots to join the stream of refugees across the borders of India and Pakistan.

On 14 August 1947, when Gandhi was busy with messages of solace and harmony in the riot-torn slums of Calcutta, the Constituent Assembly of the Dominion of India met at Delhi just before midnight. In his emotionally stirred voice, Nehru, who was to become the First Prime Minister of an Independent India, addressed the members: "At the stroke of the midnight hour, when the world sleeps, India will awake to life and freedom. A moment comes, which comes but rarely in history, when we step out from the old to the new, when the age ends, and when the soul of a nation, long suppressed, finds utterance. It is fitting at this solemn moment that we take the pledge of dedication to the service of India and her people and to the still larger cause of humanity." Nehru's words which broke the eerie silence of the sultry August-midnight brought cheers and hopes to the hearts of the millions of Indians who remained awake on that fateful night to welcome the greatest moment in their lives. In a few hours the Sun that was to rise on the eastern horizon, with a hallow of gold around it, would be so different from the Sun that rose yesterday morning! India had achieved freedom!

Postscript

So, at mid-night on 15 August 1947, after a freedom movement lasting nearly three-quarters of a century we have achieved independence through bifurcation of India. The partition created traumatic experiences for those people, particularly for the people of Bengal and the Punjab, who were affected by it. They were uprooted and displaced from their old surroundings and moorings, became hapless victims to loot and arson, robbery and murder, rape and disgrace of their women. The scene of unending flow of people fleeing the land of their birth and occupation on foot or by transport of any kind, to unknown and unfamiliar places which had suddenly become their homeland for refuge and rehabilitation, by virtue of their professed religion, was indeed a moving one. The partition thus left a burning scar among them too deep to heal and it became too bitter a pill to swallow—a nightmarish memory for those who are still alive.

The partition has ever since remained as an open wound for these people and whenever there is a new publication by a privileged member of a government claiming to throw fresh light on it, this wound is aggravated. In every country there is a rule which governs the transfer of all governmental records to its archives for use by the public after a lapse of a certain period of time, say, from 30 to 50 years. However, despite the existence of a similar rule in our country, records from the government are hardly transferred in time to our National Archives and this puts the member of a government, say, a minister or a high official, in an advantageous position to utilize such a source without verifying its authenticity from a study of other available sources, to write on a sensitive subject and come forward with a claim to reveal a secret, which is not always historically and factually correct.

In the preceding chapter, *Freedom at Midnight,* we have discussed briefly but substantially each of the developments since 1940 onwards which led to the partition of our country hastened by the Muslim League' s refusal in 1946 to join the Constituent Assembly, by the attempt of the Muslim League's ministers in the Interim Government to block its function at every stage and finally by its call for "Direct Action" which plunged the country, particularly Bengal and the Punjab, into a communal frenzy and atrocities lasting for nearly a year from August 1946 to August 1947. This forced the hands of our Congress leaders including Gandhi's and had no other alternative but to accept the Muslim League's demand for a separate homeland to save the country from an impending civil war between the two communities, the Hindus and the Muslims.

As we have already pointed out in the *Introduction,* the Muslim League which surfaced in 1906 actually owed its origin to a complex set of historical forces which could be traced to the first decade of the nineteenth century when the officials of the East India Company began to look upon the Hindus and the Muslims as two separate communities as an instrument of an administrative expediency on the eve of the passing of the Charter Act of 1813 to stall the Christian missionaries to come to India for proselytisation. The Company officials with their long administrative experience in the country feared a possible united action by them against such actions of intervention in their religion by the missionaries which could jeopardise the interests and the very existence of the Company itself.

After the transfer of power in 1858 this policy of divide and rule was carried through by the support provided to Syed Ahmed Khan's establishment of the Muhammedan Anglo-Oriental College at Aligarh in 1875 with Theodore Beck as its principal who was a proverbial hater of the Western educated Hindus and later after the first session of the Indian National Congress at Bombay in 1885, to his two nation theory of Hindus and Muslims in India, as well as by the announcement of the principle of communal representation in the Act of 1909 which provided for the separate electorates for the Muslims.

As stated in the *Introduction* earlier, the creation of the Muslim League at Dacca in 1906 in the wake of the partition of Bengal by the Nawab Salimullah Khan who was bribed by Curzon as well as its development later in the same year in December at Simla into a full-fledged political party is the climax of the policy of divide and rule pursued by the British since the beginning of the nineteenth century. The British partitioned Bengal because they saw the country as the epi-centre of most of the anti-British activities in the country. The Muslim majority in the eastern part of Bengal was pleased with the partition of Bengal as it saved them from the atrocities of the Hindu zamindars. The partition was subsequently annulled in 1911 but the Muslim League not only stayed back but grew from strength to strength and finally reached a stage when it could argue and bargain with both the government and the Congress leaders for a separate homeland for the Muslims, which it ultimately got in 1947 through "Direct Action".

Underlying all these developments leading to the partition or bifurcation of our country in August 1947 against the wishes of the majority of the Congress leaders, there are three formidable factors, often overlooked by many of us, which silently but steadily ,worked for it. The first important factor is, of course, that of number. Despite a rule of our country for nearly 650 years and every possible attempt made to convert the conquered subjects into their religion, the Muslims remained a minority group. So when demands for constitutional reforms was made to increase the number of Indian representation in the legislative councils at the very first session of the Indian National Congress, the Western educated Muslims were quick to realize that unless and until the Muslims were declared a nation within a nation they would be nowhere when such a demand for constitutional reforms was implemented in any Act for India by the British Crown. As a matter of fact, it was this very consideration of the minority status of their own community that from the very beginning of the freedom movement weighed heavily with them and lay at the root of their almost constant demand for separate electorates for their community. And their fear was apprehended and understood by the British rulers when they partitioned Bengal, and was allayed in the Morley-Minto Reforms which formed the basis of the much condemned provision on communal representation in the Act of 1909.

The second factor is of mutual hatred and distrust among the two communities for each other, generated by the Muslim invaders and conquerors who ruled our country for nearly 650 years from 1206 onwards till they were replaced by the British. The Muslim rulers wanted to convert India into Dar-ul-Islam or the land of Islam from Dar-ul-Harb or the land of unbelievers but when they failed to do it because of the sheer majority of the Hindus, they allowed the latter to exist as "Zimmis" or protected subjects who had to pay a poll tax called Jiziya which was abolished by Akbar but later reimposed by Aurangzeb. The unbelievers as "Zimmis" had no political or religious freedom and had to live with what we may call, in modem parlance, the life of a second class citizen in their own country.

With the dawn of the rule of the English East India Company in India regarded by the Court of Directors at London as an "Act of Providence" and the introduction of English education replacing Persian in 1835,this scenario changed dramatically and the position of the Muslims as rulers vis--a-vis Hindus as protected subjects gradually became reversed. The Hindus long after the spell of Persian which stunted their intellectual growth and development, culture and civilisation, were quick to understand the dynamic values and ideas of the English language. They flocked to learn and master it to their great advantage, grabbing the opportunities for employment open to them by the East India Company under Bentinck as well as by enlightening themselves with Western ideas, philosophy and culture.

The third factor is more psychological than political. In the race for learning English the Muslims were clearly outdistanced by the Hindus but the Muslims never made any serious attempt to catch up with them till Syed Ahmed Khan appeared on the scene. This is mainly because of the fact the Muslim community in India suffered from a superiority complex as the ruling class of the country for nearly 650 years, remained doggedly attached to their past culture and glory and meticulously shunned, often with contempt and disdain, the language of the people who were now not only usurping them from their past elevated positions but also were attempting to place them on the same footing with the Zimmis who they once hated so much as Kaffers or infidels.

While the British exploited the mutual hatred and distrust between the two people as Hindus and Muslims much to their advantage to pursue a policy of *divide et imperia,* it was a combination of these factors which governed and often explained most of the dramatic actions and attitudes as displayed by the majority of the Muslim leaders including Syed Ahmed Khan and Muhammad Ali Jinnah.

Thus Syed Ahmed Khan who set up his Muhammedan Anglo-Oriental College to uplift the backwardness of the Muslim community in 1875, and was very close to the first generation of the Hindu leaders of the country, quickly changed his mind after the first session of the Indian National Congress in December 1885. He reacted to the Congress Movement by organising an Educational Congress in 1886 for the Muslims, propounded his theory of two nations as far as the Hindus and the Muslims were concerned and came forward with a separate organization, United Indian Patriotic Association in 1888 for the Indian Muslims to counteract the Congress Movement and asked the Muslims not to attend any Congress session. Similarly Jinnah who had his schooling in England and was brought up with a very heavy dose of Western ideas and values was initially very close to the Western educated leaders of the Indian National Congress and shared their dream of establishing an united and independent country. However he soon realised that the Muslim leaders would have little or no impact in a decision making process to administer the country where the Hindus would be a majority in the government and when his demand for autonomous federal states for the Muslims was repeatedly thwarted by the Congress leaders, he became fully converted to the ideas of the Muslim League and not only revived Syed Ahmed's two nation theory in 1940 but also remained adamantly attached to it, much to the delight of the last British Conservative Viceroy in India, Wavell.

It is the subtle operation of these three factors that initially drove both Syed Ahmed Khan and Muhammad Ali Jinnah to the arms of the British. Initially the British tried to play them against the Congress movement to prolong their stay in the country. However, with the mounting opposition to the British rule in the country coupled with the mounting loss suffered in men and money at home as an aftermath of the Second World War and finally installment of the Labour Government in the election of July 1945 tilted the balance in favour of leaving India as early as possible and this was announced by Attlee in the House of Commons on 20 February 1947.

Assuming that the British left us an united, centralised and federal India, it could not remain so for long because of the operation of the three factors just delineated above. If Nehru accepted the grouping of the Muslim dominated areas in the Cabinet Mission Plan accepted by Jinnah in three-tier confederal structure of a government with a weak centre, it would have been a case of a *de facto* partition with the kind of internal problems which we now face from across the borders and the functioning of the weak central government would have ceased to pave way for the rise of dictatorship.

Partition of the country was thus bound to happen sooner or later and we thank god that it happened some sixty decades ago and has saved us from the kind of fate that has been almost regularly visiting our neighbours. We have our democracy, our fundamental rights and our right to change our government every five years. We are also globally known as one of the most corrupt and illiterate countries in the world. Yet at the same time we are admired for our past civilization and culture, yogas and ayurvedas, music and fine arts as well as for our modern information technology and mathematical skill. There is no use in indulging in such wishful thinking as by the present generation that the absence of partition would have saved us from an armed race, Kashmir problem, cross-border terrorism and would have bestowed on us a sound economy and a glorified top place in the world of cricket and hockey.

Select Bibliography

The Select Bibliography is meant only for those non-specialist audience who are further interested in the subject. As stated in the *Introduction*, the author has based his account primarily on *the Proceedings of the Indian National Congress (1885-1947)* as available at the Nehru Memorial Museum and Library, New Delhi, the *Contemporary Newspapers (1857-1947)* as available in the Newspapers section of the National Library, Calcutta and the *Private Papers* of the Viceroys and the Governor-Generals as available on microfilm at the National Archives of India, New Delhi and at the Nehru Memorial Museum and Library, New Delhi.

Adhikari, G., : *Pakistan and National Unity.* Bombay, 1944.

Akbar, M.J., : *Nehru, the Making of India.* London. 1988.

Andrews, C.F. and Mukherjee, Girija, : *The Rise and Growth of the Congress in India.* London, 1938.

Argov, D., : *Moderates and Extremists in the Indian Nationalist Movement.* Bombay, 1967.

Azad, Maulana Abul Kalam, : *India Wins Freedom.* Calcutta, 1988.

Banerjee, A.C., : *Indian Constitutional Documents,* 4 Vols. Calcutta, 1961.

Banerjea, Surendra Nath, : *A Nation in Making.* Calcutta, 1965.

Besant, Annie, : *How India Wrought for Freedom.* Madras, 1915.

Bose, A.C., : *Indian Revolutionaries Abroad.* Patna, 1971.

N.S. Bose, : *The Indian National Movement.* Calcutta, 1965.

Brecher, M., : *Nehru.* London, 1959.

Brown, Judith, : *Gandhi's Rise to Power.* Cambridge, 1972.

________________, :*Gandhi and Civil Disobedience.* Cambridge, 1977.

Buch, M.A., : *Rise and Growth of Indian Militant Nationalism.* Baroda, 1940.

Campbell, Johnson A., : *Mission with Mountbatten.* London, 1951.

Chandra, Bipan, Tripathi, Amales and De, Barun, : *Freedom Struggle.* Delhi, 1973.

Chatterjee, Nandalal, : *India's Freedom Struggle.* Allahabad, 1958.

Chintamani, C.Y., : *Indian Politics since the Mutiny.* Bombay, 1937.

Chirol, Valentine, : *Indian Unrest.* London, 1910.

________________, : *India.* London, 1926.

Collins, L and Lapierre, D., : *Freedom at Midnight.* Delhi, 1976.

Coupland, R., : *Constitutional Problem in India,* London, 1944.

Das, Durga (ed.), : *SardarPatel's Correspondence,* 10 vols. Abmedabad, 1971-74.

Desai, A.R., : *Social Background of Indian Nationalism.* Bombay, 1960.

Dutta, R. Palme, : *India Today.* Bombay, 1947.

Edwardes, M., : *The Last Years of British India.* London, 1963.

Gandhi, M.K., : *The Story of My Experiments with Truth.* Ahmedabad, 1927.

Ghosh, P.C., : *Indian National Congress.* Calcutta, 1960.

Ghosh, S.C., : *Indian Nationalism.* Delhi, 1985.

Gopal, S., : *Jawaharlal Nehru,* 3 Vols. Delhi, 1976-83.

___________ : *Selected Works of Jawaharlal Nehru,* 15 and 7 Vols. in old and new series respectively, Delhi, 1972-88.

Government of India, : *Terrorism in India,* 1917-36. Delhi, 1974.

Hodson, H.V., : *The Great Divide.* London, 1969.

Low, D.A. (ed.), : *Soundings in Modern South Asian History.* California, 1968.

___________ : *Congress and the Raj.* London, 1977.

___________ : *The Indian National Congress.* Delhi, 1988.

Lovett, Verney, : *A History of the Indian Nationalist Movement,* London, 1968.

McLane, J.R., : *Indian Nationalism and the Early Congress.* Princeton, 1977.

Mansergh, N. (ed.), : *Transfer of Power,* 1942-47, 9 Vols. London, 1970-73.

Majumdar, B.B., : *Militant Nationalism in India.* Calcutta, 1967.

Majumdar, R.C., : *History of the Freedom Movement in India,* 3 vols. Calcutta, 1962-64.

___________ : *The Sepoy Mutiny and the Revolt of 1857.* Calcutta, 1963.

___________ : *Struggle for Freedom,* Calcutta, 1962.

Martin, Briton, : *New India, 1885.* Bombay, 1970.

Mathur, Y.B., : *Quit India Movement.* Delhi 1979.

Mehrotra, S.R., : *The Emergence of the Indian National Congress.* Delhi, 1971.

Menon, V.P., : *Transfer of Power in India.* Delhi 1957.

__________ : *Story of Integration of Indian States.* Bombay, 1956.

Moon, Penderel, : *Divide and Quit.* London, 1961.

Moore, R.J., : *Liberalism and Indian Politics.* London, 1966.

__________ : *Crisis of Indian Unity.* Oxford, 1974.

__________ : *Churchill, Cripps and India,* Oxford, 1979.

__________ : *Escape from Empire,* Oxford, 1983.

Nanda. B.R,, : *Gokhale, the Indian Moderates and the British Raj.* Delhi, 1977.

Nehru, Jawaharlal, : *An Autobiography.* Delhi, 1962,

O'Malley, L.S.S.(ed.), : *Modern India and the West.* Oxford, 1941.

Philips, C.H. (ed.), : *Evolution of India and Pakistan.* London, 1962.

Philips, C.H. and Wainwright M.D. (ed.), : *The Partition of India. Politics and Perspectives.* London, 1970.

Prasad, Amba, : *The Indian Revolt of 1942.* Delhi, 1958.

Prased, Rajendra, : *An Autobiography.* Bombay, 1957.

Rai, Lajpat, : *Autobiographical Writings* (ed. by V.C. Joshi). Delhi, 1965.

Sarkar, Sumit, : *Swadeshi Movement in Bengal.* Delhi, 1973.

Seal, Anil, : *The Emergence of Indian Nationalism.* Cambridge, 1968.

Sen, S.N., : *Eighteen Fifty-Seven.* Delhi, 1957.

Singh Jaswant, Jinnah, : *India—Partition. Independence.* Delhi, 2009.

Sitaramaiya, P., : *History of the Indian National Congress,* 2 Vols. Bombay, 1946-47.

Symonds, R.A., : *The Making of Pakistan.* London, 1950.

Tara Chand, : *History of the Freedom Movement in India,* 4 Vols. Delhi, 1961-72.

Tendulkar, D.G, : *The Mahatma,* 8 Vols. Delhi, 1960-63.

Tomlinson, B.R., : *Indian National Congress and the Raj, 1929-42*, London, 1976.

Toye, Hugh, : *The Springing Tiger.* London, 1959.

Tripathi, Amales, : *The Extremist Challenge.* Calcutta, 1967.

Tyabji, Badr-ud-din, : *Memoirs of an Egoist,* 1907-56, Vol. 1. Delhi, 1988.

Wavell, Lord, : *The Viceroy's Journal* (ed. by Penderel Moon). Oxford, 1973.

Wolpert, Stanley, : *Tilak and Gokhale.* California, 1962.

__________ and Sisson Richard (eds.), : *Congress and Indian Nationalism, Delhi, 1988.*

Index

B

D

E

T